CHRISTIAN FAITH
in *Action*

CHRISTIAN FAITH
in *Action*

Fourteen Sermons
on Current Moral Issues

by J. B. WEATHERSPOON
J. HOWARD WILLIAMS
THEODORE F. ADAMS
CARLYLE MARNEY, and others

Compiled by
FOY VALENTINE

BROADMAN PRESS

Nashville
Tennessee

Library of Congress Card Catalog Number: 56–8672
Printed in the United States of America
5.JN56 K.S.P.

Foreword

~~~~~~~~~~~~~~~~~~~~~~~~~~~~~~~~~

Is the Christian faith practical? Is God concerned about family life? As he keeps the universe on schedule, does he deem as worthy of his consideration our problems of divorce, sex, and juvenile delinquency? Does he care about our relations with other races? Is he interested in a Christian's acceptance of responsibility as a citizen? Does it matter to him that his people daily face a multitude of perplexing moral issues? Is he touched by all the problems that surround a man in his daily work? Does Jesus Christ have a message for our day in these important areas?

This volume of sermons was prepared in the conviction that the Christian faith *is* practical, that God *is* concerned about the great moral issues with which Christians daily grapple, and that Jesus *does* have a message for our day in these significant areas.

For many years Christians have been growing in their awareness that Christianity involves not only an inward experience but also an outward expression. Their conviction has matured that man's right spiritual relationship to God imposes on him an inescapable responsibility for his fellow man. Christians have experienced a new willingness to accept the biblical teaching that a man is his brother's keeper. They have been challenged, not to discontinue their faithful emphasis on the necessity of a new birth, but to proclaim with proportionate zeal the moral and social responsibilities of the new life.

Emphasis on the practical aspect of the Christian faith needs continuing attention because moral issues are never settled "for keeps." Every generation must do battle with its own dragons. We must not—to change the figure—march seven times around Jericho and blow our trumpets at walls that fell a hundred years ago. But we *must* be alert to the enemies of God in our own time.

The wholehearted co-operation of these fourteen contributors has been most gratifying. Without exception they are extremely busy men, but their interest in and response to the idea of this project made the preparation of the volume a real joy. Each writer was free to express his personal convictions so that the sermons do not necessarily reflect the opinion of the compiler or the position of the publisher.

Here are urgent messages on marriage and the family, sex, divorce, race relations, segregation in the public schools, Christian citizenship, juvenile delinquency, honesty, covetousness, daily work, the problem of drinking, and church and state. May they challenge the preachers who read them to declare from their own pulpits some truths which they may have been neglecting. May they strengthen the moral fiber of all who read them and be used in some way by the Lord to fan the flame of a moral awakening.

Foy Valentine, *Director*
Christian Life Commission
Baptist General Convention of Texas

Dallas, Texas

Contents

Jesus Is Lord || 1

PHILIPPIANS 2:9–11

J. B. WEATHERSPOON

On a Sunday morning I sat in a crowded church at the hour of worship. There were hymns of adoration and consecration. The Scriptures were read, reminding us that God was speaking his truth and his will for mankind. The pastor prayed for us, concluding with this petition: "That our hearts may turn to him who is the only answer to the sins of men and the confusion of society." And the sermon ended with a call to surrender our hearts and lives to Jesus Christ. Thus came to us in a holy hour the picture of sin and our world's confusion, and of Christ our Lord as the only hope of redemption and peace. Song and prayer and sermon united to proclaim the faith that "Jesus Christ is Lord."

That was no unique service. Probably in every Christian congregation in the world that day Jesus was called Lord. And it was as it should be. For in the New Testament that is the pre-eminence everywhere given to him. From the angelic announcement of the birth of "Christ the Lord" to the final prayer, "Even so, come Lord Jesus," there was no name that so fittingly expressed his dignity and his right.

The simple affirmation, "Jesus is Lord," became the basic creed of the first Christians. Three names were most commonly on their lips, sometimes singly, sometimes all

1

together. He was "Jesus," a name that identified him as a man. He was "Christ," a word that expressed faith in him as the fulfilment of the messianic promise of the Old Testament. The third and highest name for him was "Lord," which proclaimed their faith in his divine nature. He was God incarnate. In him dwelt "all the fulness of the Godhead bodily." That became the keystone of all their thought of him. In its terms they interpreted his life and his death on the cross. Its reality was not only declared by the resurrection; it was really the source of the power of resurrection. Such is the faith that they preached to the world: Jesus is Lord!

Most Christians probably agree with the apostolic theology. But "Jesus is Lord" is not just a statement of faith, a theological creed; it contains a moral challenge. "Lord" means owner and ruler with the right to command. For one to say, therefore, with sincere assent that Jesus is Lord is to face a moral obligation to obey him, which cannot be refused without betraying the faith. That too is abundantly expressed in the New Testament. For one thing, it emphasizes Jesus' own assertion of his authority to command and the necessity of obedience. The Sermon on the Mount, about which there has been much questioning as to whether or not it was meant to be obeyed in the present world, concludes with the Lord's warning that to try to build a life on any other foundation is to invite disaster. The faith that Jesus sought in his disciples was more than believing something about him; it was trustful acceptance of his *rule*. He asserted the emptiness of saying "Jesus is Lord" without also obeying his word in the question, "Why call ye me Lord, Lord, and do not the things that I say?"

The New Testament makes it plain, also, that the obedience of faith is not a mere matter of keeping commandments. It goes deeper than that. To accept Jesus as Lord is to commit oneself to his interests, to receive his principles as the laws of life, to seek to enter into his attitudes and purposes.

For example, read the appeal of Paul as he wrote to the Christians at Philippi. He was discussing Christian attitudes. In the background was a situation of cross-purposes that created strife, of pride that despised others, of self-interest that ignored the welfare of others. He was trying to replace these destroyers with unity of heart, humility, and sacrificial love. How did he go about it? He simply asked them to look at Christ and answer some questions. Is there any appeal in him to you as his followers? Does he turn your hearts to faction, pride, selfishness, or to love and the sense of common life together in his Spirit, to lowliness and compassion? What do you see in him whom God has proclaimed, and whom you, his followers, have accepted as Lord? And then in matchless portraiture he told the story of Christ's self-chosen humiliation:

From the beginning He had the nature of God. Yet He did not regard equality with God as something at which He should grasp. Nay, He stripped Himself of His glory, and took on Him the nature of a bondservant by becoming a man like other men. And being recognized as truly human, He humbled Himself and even stooped to die; and that too a death on the cross. It is because of this also that God has so highly exalted Him, and has conferred on Him the Name which is supreme above every other name, in order that in the Name of JESUS every knee should bow, of beings in the highest heavens, of those on the earth, and of those in the underworld, and that every tongue should confess that JESUS CHRIST is LORD, to the glory of God the Father. PHILIPPIANS 2:5–11, WEYMOUTH

The spirit of Jesus' life, his lowliness, his love, his sacrifice of himself for all mankind—all were bound up with his lordship. God set his imprimatur upon them. They are heaven's virtues, and to bow before Jesus Christ as Lord surely must mean that they become our goals. The moral challenge of our faith is no less than this: "Let the same disposition be in you which was in Christ Jesus."

The early Christians set no limit upon the authority of Christ. When they said "Jesus is Lord," they meant that his words, his deeds, his principles, his traits became the law, the spirit, the goal of living. They counted themselves as his slaves. "Jesus is Lord" meant that his authority was greater than tradition and custom, and when these were in conflict with his will, they were willing for his sake to suffer the scorn of the world. They meant that he was greater than the gods of the pagan world. They meant that he was Lord over Caesar, and they accepted persecution and martyrdom rather than deny him. They gave to his lordship a moral meaning that penetrated every area of life with its challenge to follow him.

That is New Testament doctrine, boldly accepted, consistently followed, and courageously preached. To some extent the lordship of Jesus is today a tenet of all who call themselves Christians. The trouble is that so many see only one side of the coin. Some accept the moral challenge of his life and teachings, and commit themselves to his way of life, but they do not worship him as the eternal Son of God. He is *only* a great teacher and saint. Others accept him as God incarnate, who in his death purchased our redemption, and in his resurrection was proclaimed the Lord over sin and death. They worship him as God and trust him to save their souls, *but* in their worship, while they feel great exaltation of spirit, they fail to hear the moral challenge of his righteousness and sacrificial, redemptive love. Faith for them is something less than a self-commitment to obey him, something less than letting him live in us and express himself through us in our communities. That sort of faith sees him as the Saviour of the soul, but not as the Lord of conscience in determining attitudes and behavior.

Neither of these interpretations is enough; both have failed to grasp the full reality of his lordship. One takes him off the throne; the other keeps him on a throne, but afar off, giving him but limited voice in the guidance of life. The time is upon us when we must accept the full lordship of Jesus in our lives now. Our lives like our creeds must proclaim "Jesus Christ is Lord."

It is our partial acceptance of the lordship of Christ that makes so embarrassing the question often met in our day: "If Jesus Christ is Lord, why is all this?" What "all this" is, need not be described at any length. War, and the spiritual evil that produces it; political and economic corruption, and the ambition and avarice that call them just; class and racial hatred, and the pride and love of mastery that foment them; a thousand varieties of social evils that write their black records of divorce, crime, delinquency, drunkenness, gambling, and vileness in the pages of the history we are making—why all these things if Jesus Christ is the Lord who cannot fail?

The answer of some Christians is that Christ has not failed but that, as Chesterton put it, the world has found him difficult and has not tried him. But that is a slippery answer. It is a boomerang; we throw it out to a puzzled and unbelieving world, and it returns to indict us. "True, the world has not tried him, but *you* have tried him. Are you a demonstration of the measure of his power? Why are these things still among *you?*" And we face the sad fact that Christianity is far from having convinced the world that Christ is worth trying as a purifier of life. We can find no satisfaction in the answer that Christ has not been tried. It is our condemnation.

"If Jesus Christ is Lord, then why all this?" Another answer to this question says frankly that the social and moral conditions of society, although they testify to the power of sin, in no way disprove the supreme lordship of Christ. He is the Lord of history and in the end he will conquer. All things are working according to his purpose. That does not satisfy those who "seek after a sign," but it expresses the basic faith and hope of Christians, that one day he will be universally acknowledged, and every tongue shall confess that "Jesus Christ is Lord to the glory of God the Father."

Unfortunately many Christians cherish this faith and hope in a complacency that takes them out of the moral and spiritual struggle. Too many of us have let the logic of our predestination doctrines relieve us of participation in the redemptive work of Christ. We have said, "If it is God's business, it is not ours." Our answer to the world's question is good, but our logic too easily quenches the Spirit that stirs us to throw ourselves into God's battle against all destroying evil.

For example, the time was in America and among Baptists when the doctrine of election and the evangelistic and missionary spirit were in violent conflict. The Primitive Baptists held the doctrine in a form that made evangelism, missions, and education unnecessary, if not an impertinence. The argument was that the salvation of a soul was wholly God's business, and he would accomplish it according to his own electing grace. Surely if anything is wholly God's prerogative, it is regeneration. But Christ's command to witness and teach could not be wholly forgotten. In some the love of lost men and the impulse to persuade and plead with them cried out against the logic of the dogma. Those whom "missionary Baptists" own as fathers were bold enough to reinterpret the doctrine of election so as to include the divine use of human instrumentality in preparing and persuading men to believe. It was an unhappy chapter in Baptist history, but today we rejoice that it happened; for it was the beginning of a great spiritual revival, the ushering in of a period of evangelism and missions that is still increasing in momentum, and the awakening in our denomination of the sense of mission that has become a strong bond of unity.

Another example of how we have permitted our faith in the lordship of Jesus Christ to limit Christian action is by so interpreting the future of human society and the kingdom of God as to make any effort to establish a righteous social order as either unnecessary or futile. Here again a doctrine of predestination (social predestination) is the starting point. "What happens to human society is wholly in God's hands." And with easy logic many go on to add "and not man's."

This idea is expressed in several doctrinal forms, one of which is that social righteousness will be achieved by the process of social evolution. It believes that God moves by a law of progress which serves his purpose. Under its operation there is taking place a gradual improvement of the human spirit and human relations. Even our selfishness by the power of an invisible hand is converted into ultimate social good. One day the earth will be ready for the kingdom of heaven. Therefore, we need not be too greatly disturbed by "all this" for it, too, will pass, and on the ash heap of the twentieth century God will build a better tomorrow.

Another theory goes further but in the opposite direction. It repudiates the law of social progress and avers that society is doomed. Jesus shall reign, but only by a destroying judgment that will fall suddenly upon the world. It claims that human society is irredeemably evil. Neither God nor man can make men brotherly in institutional relations. The only way righteousness will ever triumph on earth will be by a heaven-sent catastrophic judgment. What then can Christianity do? To try to change social attitudes, purify social relations, to reconstruct society at a high moral level is utterly futile. Forty days and then the judgment!

Unlike Jonah, men of this view have failed to discover that behind his proclamation of judgment is God's heart of mercy, ready to set aside judgment in his desire to save our Babylon's men and civilization if men will but hear his voice and come under his rule. They have let a form of doctrine stifle the love of mankind that longs to see injustice, oppression, cruelty, hatred, war, and confusion banished from human relations. To try to save society from its evils is not to deny a final judgment; it is not an effort to build a tower of Babel; it is not an effort to substitute a good America for the kingdom of God. It is no substitute for the gospel. It is rather a response to the Spirit of our Lord, who chose us and set us in the midst of men to be instruments of righteousness and peace. It is time again for us to open our doctrine to let the Spirit in—the Spirit of love and healing and cleansing and rebuilding for the peace and progress of human society.

Still another form of faith hinders Christian action in

social reconstruction by restricting the rule of Christ to certain areas and relations of life. To this way of thinking an organization like the Southern Baptist Convention, or its Christian Life Commission, is going beyond the requirements of Christ when it invokes the authority of his teachings and Spirit to criticize or approve the moral aspects of public questions. Too long have we consented to leave politics, economic life, and social situations outside any serious Christian concern. Too long we have been servants of the status quo and of custom, instead of obeying the principles of our Lord. We must come back to the New Testament faith that Christ is Lord above all other claimants to our obedience, that his will must prevail over self-interest, over the common social morality, over tradition, over Caesar, wherever they challenge his authority. If we would be wholly Christian, we must let him rule our actions in every area.

Let us, then, lay hold of all the truth of Christ's lordship. Let us believe that all depends on God, that the destiny of individuals and of society is in his hands, that there is a law of progress, that there must be a final judgment of all revolting evil. But let us believe also in the divine employment of human personalities, that he sheds abroad his love in the hearts of men, that his spirit stirs men to love and lift and to bring purity and justice into the life of the world. It is not a matter of building or establishing the kingdom of God on earth; it is a matter of accepting our social responsibility as citizen-Christians. It is a matter of making Christ the Lord of conscience and of all our living.

What can we accomplish? Who knows? Who knows what God can do with a host committed to the lordship of Christ? Confidently leaving the fruits of our obedience in his hands, this we can do. We can become laborers together with God in making a better world, spiritually, socially, physically. We can in the name of our Lord refuse to leave the welfare of our nation to the wisdom of un-believers. We can stand in the vanguard, rather than "drag our feet," in social movements and moral reforms that make for the improvement of life. We can seize the op-portunity of this changing age in which we live to bring Christian principles to bear upon the social decisions that are being made.

We can assert in our living what surely we have learned from our Lord: that truth is better than falsehood, that honesty is better than dishonesty, that fairness is better than advantage, that love is better than hate, that to lift is better than to cast down, that to help is better than to oppress, that peace is better than war, that to be a brother is better than to be a master, that humility is better than pride, that to suffer persecution for righteousness' sake is better than to compromise with evil. What can these things do in the midst of "all this"? Who knows? We do know that Jesus is Lord, and that the world waits for men like Caleb of old who "wholly followed the Lord" while others quaked before giants.

Christian Citizenship || 2

PHILIPPIANS 1:27; 3:20

J. HOWARD WILLIAMS

> Breathes there a man, with soul so dead,
> Who never to himself hath said,
> This is my own, my native land!

So wrote Sir Walter Scott in "Lay of the Last Minstrel." Love of country is one of the noblest sentiments that can stir the human heart.

Van Dyke wrote a beautiful little poem under the title "America for Me." After mentioning various countries and marvelous sites which he had seen abroad, he closed by saying, "It's home again! Home again! America for me!" The love of country, the patriotic sentiments which surged through his heart found expression in his beautiful little poem.

An American Negro soldier, returning from World War I, looked up to the face of the Statue of Liberty as his ship moved into the port of New York. With real fervor and a touch of humor, he addressed the great statue: "Well, lady, if you ever see my face again, you will have to turn around."

It was Paul who said, "I am a citizen of no mean city." There is evidence of civic pride, and I like the bold declaration, "I am a citizen." Someone is said to have rebuked Dwight L. Moody for his positive position on moral issues, saying, "After all, are you not a citizen of heaven?" To this

11

he replied, "Indeed I am a citizen of heaven, but right now I vote in Cook County, Illinois."

Christian citizenship must be far more than pride in one's city, state, or nation. The Christian must not permit himself to enjoy the blessings of his native land without assuming his citizenship responsibilities. Christian citizenship does not allow him to be a civic hitchhiker. There are no free rides for the conscientious Christian.

I. THE HARVEST OF POOR CITIZENSHIP

Good government is no accident. Someone has remarked that one of the greatest scandals of America is the "bad citizenship of good men." To earn this reputation, good men need not be actively allied with the enemies of good government; they need only to be passive, indifferent to community problems. In this field, as in so many others, the sins of omission are as unfortunate in their results as the sins of commission. The enemies of good government are active, aggressive, and successful where good men are unwilling to stand up and be counted.

While the low levels of life are not confined to the cities, conditions there are often accentuated. Frequently there is corruption, expressing itself in organized crime. Bootlegging, the sale and use of other narcotics, gangsterism in general, graft among peoples in high and low places, even the corruption of courts and the channels of justice, are not uncommon.

The good people of Galveston, Texas, were not aroused until conditions in their city became notorious. The city administration had boldly declared itself by saying that Galveston was to be an open city. Prostitution, gambling, and the free use of liquor were not only to be countenanced but actually encouraged. Finally, the business interests awoke to the realization that the gangsters had taken over. The money they filched from the public was not used to pave the streets, build better schools, encourage the growth of the city. Business and civic leaders found that the good people of Texas were actually avoiding Galveston; they were unwilling to take their families into a notorious community.

Therefore, legitimate businesses fell upon hard times, while those who operated those businesses were left to pay taxes from their dwindling receipts. A beautiful island of tropical glory, with miles of natural beaches, flowering oleanders, and modern hotels and motels, was being by-passed by multitudes of people going elsewhere for vacations. The better people of Galveston were rudely awakened to the fact that sin does not pay; that anything which is morally wrong cannot be economically profitable. They have at last assumed the responsibilities of Christian citizenship and are seeking to do something about them.

The race track interests came into Texas, and their operation was contingent upon pari-mutuel gambling. The state was not rid of this evil until the business interests awoke to the fact that embezzlement was becoming common, and that murders and suicides were frequent. The credit men of legitimate business enterprises complained that women shoppers demanded that advances of cash be posted on their bills as merchandise sold in order that their unsuspecting husbands would not know they were gambling on the races. When the economic forces were ready to join with the moral forces, victory came in short order, and the state got rid of this evil.

II. REWARDS OF GOOD CITIZENSHIP

It would be easy to talk like Pollyanna about the rewards of good citizenship. One can be realistic, however, by just stating that good citizenship produces good government, and no government can be better than the average level of its citizens makes possible.

The first requisite of a good community is good men and women—people who are fundamentally honest in character and intelligently aware of the privileges and responsibilities of citizenship.

When Paul declared he was a citizen of no mean city, he may have had in mind its size, its commercial and cultural stature. Good citizens are concerned about all that affects their community, good and bad—even the breeding places of mosquitoes, unhealthy congestion in tenement houses, poorly paved streets, inadequate school facilities, poor salaries for teachers, men of mediocre ability and dwarfed consciences in places of government, or any other of a thousand unfortunate things which may exist in any community.

On the other hand, how fortunate it is when people realize that there is more to life than meat, raiment, fat bank balances, and gilt-edged bonds in safety deposit boxes. In addition to the necessities for the welfare of a community, such as police and fire protection, good citizenship would require one to be interested in adequate playgrounds for children, beautiful parks, and a community library in keeping with the size and ability of the citizenship. Good citizens should support good entertainment, art exhibits, the development of schools of higher learning within reach of the people.

Good citizenship involves participation in good government. Democracy is the highest form of government yet developed by man. We have it as a treasure purchased by the blood of millions, but it will last only as long as others are willing to live for it. Good citizens recognize the inescapable obligation to support it by paying taxes, by voting intelligently and unselfishly, by serving on juries, and, at times, by serving in offices as volunteer workers or as paid servants of the government. The world-famed English historian, Arnold J. Toynbee, has focused his discriminating mind on this subject and says:

Democracy is another leaf from the book of Christianity, which has also, I fear, been torn out and, while perhaps not misread, has certainly been half emptied of meaning by being divorced from its Christian context and secularized; and we have obviously, for a number of generations past, been living on spiritual capital, I mean clinging to Christian practice without possessing the Christian belief—and practice unsupported by belief is a wasting asset, as we have suddenly discovered, to our dismay, in this generation.

I know a grand old man now approaching ninety years of age who has spent his lifetime as a country preacher. He has baptized hundreds of people. He was pastor of one church for forty years, being elected annually. He has been interested in everything that has affected his community. The first good roads in his county started in a conference in his home. When rumors began to spread that bootleggers were infesting his neighborhood, he organized a group which quietly raised a fund with which a detective was employed. Violators were brought to justice, and the community was rid of them. As a result of the good citizenship of this leader and others who joined with him, land values rose in the community, farms were sought out by people who wanted to live in an area where there was a good brick school building, a splendid church, an all-weather road to the county seat, and a healthy atmosphere in which to bring up their children.

III. THE CHRISTIAN MOTIVE NECESSARY

Some years ago a group of leaders from a strong agricultural college requested a conference with some religious leaders. "We have a real problem," they said. "We know how to farm, how to raise fine cattle, horses, and poultry. We know how to analyze, conserve, and terrace the land. Our problem is that we do not know how to lead farmers to do the same thing. It is one thing to teach them the facts; it is another thing to inspire them to action. We need to tie in the responsibilities of good farming with religion. The farmers need to recognize they are sinning against God and unborn generations to let their soil wash away."

The need for Christian citizenship is obvious. But we will not produce better citizens until men and women come to realize that good citizenship for a Christian is obligatory. It is not optional. We have numerous entreaties and even commands on this subject in the Word of God.

In John 17 Jesus prayed "not that thou shouldest take them out of the world, but that thou shouldest keep them from the evil." He did not want his friends to be taken out of the world. Rather he wanted them to be the salt of the earth to season and preserve life. He wanted them to be the light of the world to illumine its darkness. He wanted them to move among men, to be *in* the world but not *of* the world in the sense of participating in its spirit and accepting its compromises. He sent them out to witness both by the word of their testimony and by the manner of their lives.

This same general sentiment pervades the entire New Testament. Paul wrote to the Philippians, "Our conversation is in heaven." The word translated "conversation" means citizenship or commonwealth. Thus, the passage can well be: "Our citizenship is in heaven." Moffatt has translated it: "We are a colony of heaven." A Christian is both a pilgrim of earth and a citizen of heaven. Paul wanted the Philippian Christians to recognize that as heavenly citizens they should exemplify the spirit of the kingdom of heaven in their earthly conduct. In writing on this passage long ago Augustine suggested that "with the body we walk about on earth; with the heart we dwell in heaven."

The Philippians were subject, however, to the Roman government. They were subject to its laws. They were influenced by its ideals, its spirit, and its program. The apostle suggested that the Christians there recognize themselves as a colony of heaven planted in a pagan city to be at once a demonstration and a revelation of God's will for men. A New Testament church is a body of believers who in honor will prefer one another, who in love, care, and concern are to watch over one another in times of sickness or distress, and who will courageously reveal to a pagan world how that world can live in peace and harmony.

Exhortations to uprightness of life and worthiness of walk before the people are strong in the New Testament. Paul urged the Ephesians to "walk worthy of the vocation wherewith ye are called." And to the Philippians he wrote: "Let nothing be done through strife or vainglory; but in lowliness of mind let each esteem other better than themselves. Look not every man on his own things, but every man also on the things of others. Let this mind be in you which was also in Christ."

The entire twelfth chapter of Romans is a practical exhortation to worthy Christian citizenship on the part of God's people, and the thirteenth chapter begins, "Let every soul be subject unto the higher powers. For there is no power but of God: the powers that be are ordained of God." Verse 7 advises, "Render therefore to all their dues: tribute to whom tribute is due; custom to whom custom; fear to whom fear; honour to whom honour."

In addition to all else, Christians should pray for their fellow citizens and for their government's leaders. Such is suggested in 1 Timothy 2:1–4.

I exhort, therefore, that, first of all, supplications, prayers, intercessions, and giving of thanks, be made for all men; for kings, and for all that are in authority; that we may lead a quiet and peaceable life in all godliness and honesty. For this is good and acceptable in the sight of God our Saviour; who will have all men to be saved and to come unto the knowledge of the truth.

It would seem that the burden of this whole passage is found in the fourth verse. The redeeming heart of God is often exposed throughout the Scriptures. All that we are urged to do is based on God's intention for "all men to be saved and to come unto the knowledge of the truth."

In fact, the reasons for, and motivations to, good citizenship are multitudinous. One could use a type of selfishness as a motive inasmuch as good citizenship, like virtue, is its own reward. A sense of satisfaction, a growth in the heavenly graces of life inevitably result when a person is a good citizen. Every area and avenue of life is better where men are conscientious citizens, mindful of their duty to God and to men. Our homes are safer and society more secure; our economic relations are on a higher level; our political life is on a firmer basis; our cultural life is encouraged; our religious life flourishes in it all. Those who are born from above ought to permit the grace of God to continue to flow into their hearts that it might flow into that gracious living and into that Christian citizenship intended by our Lord for all men.

Respectable Thieves

Exodus 20:15

CHARLES WELLBORN

Some years ago the cover of the *Saturday Evening Post* showed a sweet old lady buying a Thanksgiving turkey from a fat, friendly butcher. Remember? The artist, Norman Rockwell, managed to convey, through warmth of color and wealth of detail, the atmosphere of good living and neighborliness. The turkey was being weighed on the butcher's scale. On one side of the counter stood the woman; on the other, the butcher. Both had their eyes riveted on the weight indicator, and in each pair of eyes was an expression of secret delight. Cautiously, the fat, friendly butcher had his big right thumb placed on the scales behind the turkey, pressing them down. On the opposite side the sweet old lady's chubby forefinger was underneath the scales, pressing them up. Each was unaware of the other's deception; each thought an advantage had been gained. Norman Rockwell, with tongue in cheek, could philosophize through his paintbrush that sin cancels itself out and that nothing is ultimately gained.

While such a situation has its comic aspect, it is basically tragic. The two people involved were good, decent people. The woman could be an active member of the woman's missionary organization in her church, while the butcher might be the president of his Sunday school class. Neither would be willing to admit that he had done anything seri-

19

ously wrong. Yet both were violating the Eighth Commandment of the moral law of God, as it is summed up for us in the Old Testament. Both were guilty under the precept: "Thou shalt not steal."

I. OUR HONESTY COMPROMISED

For too many years to count, parents have been teaching their children the familiar adage, "Honesty is the best policy." Schools stress the value of fair play. Civic clubs include integrity among their watchwords. Does it seem a bit strange that, in spite of all our emphasis on honesty, we still live in a grossly dishonest world? Mature thought will convince us that it is not strange at all. It takes more than slogans to change character. The very people to whom we preach and teach honesty look about them to see, at least on the surface of things, actual life situations which seem to indicate that dishonesty is the best policy. Under such circumstances, moral confusion is inescapable. Dishonest men rise to positions of wealth and power, and they appear to be happy in it all. Ethics suffer under the pressure of monetary gain or the search for prestige. No wonder that George Bernard Shaw could cynically remark, "I am afraid that we must make the world honest before we can honestly say to our children that honesty is the best policy."

At the root of this moral confusion lies the compromise which almost all of us have made in the matter of honesty. Life offers a hundred subtle ways to be dishonest; a thousand ways in which we can be minor thieves and still retain respectability; a multitude of ways in which we can steal and never run afoul of the law. Here, for most men, are the real temptations. It is not that most of us are tempted to rob a bank and, in that obvious way, violate the Eighth Commandment. Rather, the area of weakness is that of the myriad of border-line decisions—little things which compromise our honesty. Our children, seeing their parents preach honesty on the one hand, and practice dishonesty on the other, are morally frustrated. Who can blame them?

This is no new problem. Rather, it is as old as the human race. Dishonest transactions and underhand dealings were common in the days of the Old Testament. God made it clear in the Ten Commandments that honesty is fundamental in putting life on the right plane. "From thunderous Sinai, where Moses entered into the secrets of the most High, there came the solemn injunction, 'Thou shalt not steal,' and wherever truth and right have led the way there echoes in the calm of sober thought, 'Thou shalt not steal.' " [1]

But as men have violated other laws of God, they have also violated this one. "Dishonesty is a prevailing sin among us today, assuming various and sundry forms, but bearing always the same iniquitous mark. Sometimes it is material and practical, sometimes social and economic, sometimes intellectual and spiritual, but always personal and persistent. It frequently exists in the least suspected places, now veiled in the white robe of charity, now clothed in the brilliance of philanthropy, at times halfhidden in the dim light of religion, but deadly wherever it is." [2] We need—each of us—to return to an emphasis upon the meaning, the purpose, and the implications of the Eighth Commandment.

[1] John C. Slemp, *Twelve Laws of Life* (Philadelphia: Judson Press, 1950), pp. 71–72.
[2] *Ibid.*, p. 72.

II. THE BASIS OF GOD'S LAW

What is the basis of God's law forbidding dishonesty? It is important to note, first of all, that the law carries with it the clear idea that God recognizes the right and need of private ownership of property. The commandment assumes that there are some things which do not rightfully belong to an individual. If all things are held in common, as the radical communist advocates, then no theft is possible. If no one owns anything, no one can steal anything. Over against this concept, the Eighth Commandment emphasizes the dignity of ownership.

Such dignity is a recurring biblical theme. In the first chapter of Genesis, God gave to Adam the right to have dominion over every living thing. That dominion carried with it rights of ownership. There was moral purpose in this action of God. The man who owns his own home is more alert to civic responsibility, in general, than the man who does not. A man who owns something has a bigger stake in society and is challenged to be a better man for it. One has only to read his history and visualize the streets of imperial Rome, crowded with an aggressive mob—a mob that owned nothing—crying out for bread and circuses—uncontrollable, fickle, dangerous. The man who owns no property too frequently has no sense of responsibility either.

God not only recognizes the dignity of ownership; he also recognizes its dangers. Property ownership is a good thing only so long as a man remembers that people are more important than property—only so long as a man recalls that the possession of more property than someone else does not entitle him to rights and privileges at the expense of another person. It is the right of ownership which creates the problem of honesty among men—and toward God.

III. BASIC HONESTY AMONG RICH AND POOR

Jesus talked often about people who had failed to recognize the necessity for basic honesty. He described a man who had more property than he knew what to do with. And so the man talked to himself, "Isn't this fine? What shall I do now? I will replace my old barns with larger ones so that I can keep what I have accumulated. And I will say to my soul, 'Look out for yourself, soul. I'll take care of you later.'" But God said, "You fool, tonight you must give an accounting of your soul." Jesus was saying that first things must be put first. He was teaching that a man ought to watch carefully lest his sense of values become distorted—lest he begin to live dishonestly before both man and God.

To the man who already has wealth, dishonesty most often expresses itself in selfishness. Jesus looked deep into the souls of men and said with tragic truth, "How terribly difficult it is for a rich man to find his way to heaven!" Why? Because there is something basically wrong with being wealthy? No, not in the Christian philosophy. Rather, because the devil has abundant opportunity to tempt a man to become so selfish and so self-satisfied that he is not willing to pay the price for heaven. One of the most pathetic and heart-rending incidents in the entire New Testament is the story of the attractive, wealthy young man who wanted sincerely to know the one way to the highest good—eternal life. Jesus looked at him with penetrating gaze, seeing him for what he was, a worshiper of property. Jesus pointed him to the one way he could free himself from the slavery of his wealth, "Sell what you have and give to the poor; then come and follow me." That was the secret of his difficulty: his was a property-centered life. His allegiance to wealth was so strong he could not break it. Therefore, "he went away sorrowful: for he had great possessions."

"But," you may ask, "how was the rich young man dishonest? How can you say he violated the Eighth Commandment?" No indication is given that he had obtained his wealth dishonestly. He probably inherited it. His sin was the sin of hoarding, the sin of selfishness, the sin of allegiance to the money-god, the sin of failing to share with his fellow men in need. This is fundamental dishonesty.

But it is not alone the wealthy man who falls into the snare of the tempter along this line. The poor man, too, wants that which he does not have. Sometimes those who do not have wealth want it so badly that they are willing to do something dishonest in order to get it. Looking at the rich man, they say with a sneer, "I know how you got your money. You either inherited or stole it. Therefore, any method I can use to get it away from you is all right." Of course, many rich people have inherited their money, but a man has a right to pass his property on to his heirs. And some rich men have stolen part of their wealth. But there are many, many of them who have worked hard and honestly to obtain it. The fact that one man has much and that another has little does not justify the second man in stealing from the first.

The man who said that poverty was a blessing did not think the problem through. Poverty appears a blessing only to those who are not poor. Poverty may be the starting point for a gnawing, consuming desire for material things which will lead a man to try to get something for nothing, and to do it dishonestly. It is an interesting fact that most of the gambling in America is done by poor people—people who are trying to get something they want, and something they do not think they can get in any other way. Though they know they live in a world where a man reaps exactly what he sows, they persuade themselves that they are exceptions to the rule. The other fellow may get caught—not they! And so our gambling bill is more than six billion dollars a year. Few of those who gamble recognize that the gambler and the thief are twin brothers. Even those who gamble on the pin-ball machines or the football game cards are striving to get something for nothing, a form of theft. Both the thief and the gambler pride themselves on outsmarting somebody else and getting without labor that for which someone else has sweated.

Yes, the poor are as much in danger as the rich of violating this commandment of God's law. Those who make up today's respectable thieves are a cosmopolitan group, drawn from every rank of society and social standing.

IV. MODERN METHODS OF STEALING

But let us be more specific. How are we violating the Eighth Commandment? I think we can divide our violations into two groups. Some violate by aggressive, positive theft; others, by passive theft.

The definition of theft is to take, in any way, that which rightly belongs to another. Aggressively and positively we steal through *misrepresentation*. To overcharge for services rendered, to disguise the quality of goods sold, to violate the specific biblical injunction, "Thou shalt not have divers weights and measures"—all these are theft by misrepresentation. All men are entitled to a square deal. "Let the buyer beware" cannot be the slogan of the Christian seller. Unless there is a real honesty in business transactions, business will eventually collapse on every front.

Is it too painful a point to mention here the question of honesty in such prosaic matters as income tax reports? The Christian contradicts his own testimony when he cheats, falsifies, or misrepresents a tax return. To argue that thousands of others do the same thing is no justification. Dishonesty is the same, no matter how popular it may be.

Again, one may steal by taking *undue and unfair advantage of another's weakness, need, or ignorance.* Such was the method which Jacob used in securing the birthright of his older brother, Esau. He traded Esau a mess of pottage —a bowl of beans—for his birthright. Legally, the deal was binding, but before God, Jacob was a thief. To use the power of wealth or circumstance in order to obtain for oneself that which belongs to another may be legally correct, but it is not morally right. To force a man into such a position that he can do nothing else but sell property for less than it is worth is thievery, pure and simple.

There is a third method of real, though respectable, theft. It occurs in *withholding from another human being his rightful due.* The principle of a fair day's pay for a fair day's work ought to be fundamental in the dealings of employers with employees. Just as basic is the reverse principle: a fair day's work for a fair day's pay. Jeremiah the prophet preached: "Woe unto him . . . that useth his neighbour's services without wages, and giveth him not for his work" (Jer. 22:13). Here is the root of some of the most grievous troubles of our nation today. I believe in labor unions, but I regret the necessity for them. Labor unions came into existence, for the most part, because they represented the one way in which the worker could get a fair deal from his employer. Today, forgetting the reason for their beginning, some labor unions have reversed the process and are oppressing the employer and failing to give him in labor that to which he is entitled. Beyond and behind the labor-management controversies of today is the need for a return to simple honesty in the dealings of men, one with another. It is utterly amazing, in the relatively few instances in which it has been tried, to see how the spirit of Christ, applied by consecrated employers and consecrated employees, has solved labor-management difficulty. There ought to be a crusade, led by Christian businessmen and Christian laboring men, for a return to the days when a man's word was his bond.

Practical instances of the violation of the Eighth Commandment could be multiplied beyond number. Among Christians, perhaps the most prevalent breach of honesty is in our relationship to God. To fail to face seriously one's stewardship obligations is a species of dishonesty. The words of the prophet Malachi, unpleasant as they are, need to sound in the sanctuaries of our souls: "Will a man rob God? Yet ye have robbed me. But ye say, wherein have we robbed thee? In tithes and offerings" (3:8). We are prone to forget that all we have comes from God and that we are stewards of our material possessions. God holds us responsible for how we handle our property. If we are selfish with God, the creator and owner, then we are dishonest.

V. VICTORY OVER DISHONESTY

"Thou shalt not steal." Here is the word of the Lord. Here is a prevailing sin in the lives of many. What is the secret of victory over sin? As in every other area of life, the secret lies, not in fighting in our own power—gritting our teeth while we say, "I will not steal"—but in full surrender of will and mind and spirit to the overcoming power of the living Christ. To be a Christian, in the fullest sense, is not simply to surrender one's soul to Christ in faith for salvation. It is also to surrender one's character, one's integrity, one's honesty to him. When he is Lord of all of life, he gives of his strength where we are weakest. In that strength we can live the honest—the more abundant—life.

Beware of Covetousness! | 4

Luke 12:13–21

ARTHUR B. RUTLEDGE

The pathway of history is marred by the woeful wrecks produced by covetousness. It was covetousness that made Achan appropriate a portion of the plunder of Jericho, and bring disgrace upon the people of God. It was covetousness that caused David to commit the double sins of adultery and murder. It was covetousness that led Gehazi to follow Naaman and seek clothing and cash—and find leprosy—after his master, Elisha, had declined the gifts. It was covetousness that barred the door to the kingdom of God when the rich young ruler knocked. It was covetousness that forever marked the wise and prosperous farmer as a fool. It was covetousness that led Judas Iscariot to sell his Lord for a handful of money. It was covetousness that caused Ananias and Sapphira to lie to the Holy Spirit and bring death upon themselves and shame upon the church.

Therefore, it is no little wonder that the Bible should abound in warnings against covetousness. Only one other sin is more often warned against in the Bible: the sin of unbelief. The Ten Commandments, which conclude with the warning against covetousness, include at least one other commandment which would be needless except for covetousness: "Thou shalt not steal."

29

I. THE CHARACTER OF COVETOUSNESS

Covetousness is an inward sin; it is basically "the desire to possess." It may apply to worthy objects: "Covet earnestly the best gifts" (1 Cor. 12:31). Sin enters when this desire to possess centers upon that which we cannot lawfully obtain, upon that which we do not need and cannot use, upon that to which we have no right, or upon anything which will be harmful to others, to our own well being, or to God and our relations with him. The commandment against covetousness recognizes the right of private ownership and forbids the desire for unlawful, unbrotherly, and unspiritual ownership.

The Old Testament furnishes a vivid example of covetousness and its result in the story of Ahab and Naboth's vineyard. When Naboth refused to sell the land, the king was heavyhearted. His wife, the notorious Jezebel, discovered what had happened and immediately set in motion a plan which ended with Naboth's murder. As Ahab moved in to take possession of the much wanted vineyard, the prophet of God, Elijah, also moved in, with a message of severe denunciation. There was nothing wrong with Ahab's desire to own and his offer to buy Naboth's vineyard. There was nothing wrong with Naboth's refusal to sell. But there was terrible sin when this insistent "desire to possess" was allowed to run wild instead of being suppressed or replaced, and it produced woeful consequences.

Covetousness is also an ugly sin. Every sin, if we could only see it as God sees it, would be repulsive to us. Some sins are obviously ugly—such as drunkenness, lewdness, profanity, lying, and stealing. But there are other sins in which one may engage and at the same time maintain the respect and even the honor of the majority of his fellow men. It is so with covetousness.

The Bible itself makes plain that God counts covetousness to be a grave sin. It is classified with the most forbidding of immoral acts. The apostle Paul lists covetousness along with fornication, adultery, idolatry, stealing, drunkenness, dishonesty in business (1 Cor. 5:11; 6:10), and goes so far as to declare that covetousness itself is idolatry (Eph. 5:5; Col. 3:5). The apostle Peter revealed the same attitude as he included this sin of covetousness in a sickening description of "them that walk after the flesh in the lust of uncleanness" (2 Peter 2:10–16).

It is high time for us to realize that the grasping, selfish, materialistic spirit which controls so many people in our society today, and even in our churches, and which confronts every one of us, is an ugly and awful sin in the sight of God and ought to be so in our sight. If Bobby Burns could plead,

> Oh wad some powr the giftie gie us
> To see oursels as others see us

we shall do well to pray, "O God, the power give us, to see ourselves as Thou dost see us."

Let us observe also that covetousness is a destructive sin. In writing to young Timothy the apostle Paul warned against this consuming desire to possess: "But they that will be rich fall into temptation and a snare, and into many foolish and hurtful lusts, which drown men in destruction and perdition" (1 Tim. 6:9).

Most of us need not look far to find some who have vowed that they would prosper financially whatever the cost. There are such men who have worked early and late, neglecting family and friends, body and soul, and have succeeded in reaching their financial goals. But for such success they have paid an exorbitantly high price.

The prosperous farmer in Jesus' parable was a success

in the eyes of men, but for his full barns and his financial security he paid a terrific price. When men come to the point that they are dominated by the desire for wealth, dependence upon self is substituted for dependence upon God, humility is replaced by pride, vital interest in eternal things vanishes, faith falters, and eternal separation from God ensues.

II. THE CAUSES OF COVETOUSNESS

The emphasis of our society is strongly in the direction of making material goods our life goal. The unfailing American emphasis upon conveniences and comforts, cash and security, is felt by every one of us. In fact, we have gone so far in our worship of material possessions that, as Dr. Leslie D. Weatherhead has put it, we regard the man of great possessions with awe, we defer to his opinions, we are very careful not to cross him, even though it may be that he has less mental ability and spiritual perception than many of those who thus respect him. The pressures of our day are so strongly in this direction that the person who completely avoids the sin of covetousness must be rare indeed.

Spiritual blindness is evident as another of the causes of covetousness. It is because we are blind to the real values of life that we are so easily led to pursue the counterfeit values. Because material things are so necessary to life we are the more vulnerable to the temptation of covetousness. We have the difficult problem of having to work for a living and at the same time avoid making money and land, stocks and bonds ends in themselves.

Jesus never discounted the reality of physical needs. He did insist that physical things can never supply the deep wants of our lives. Hear him as he declared: "Man shall not live by bread alone, but by every word that proceedeth out of the mouth of God" (Matt. 4:4). Bread is necessary —material things are needed—but they can never supply the soul's deep needs. Here is the fundamental error of everyone who covets: things are made primary, and souls secondary, or worse. All this is true in the face of the Master's penetrating question: "For what shall it profit a man, if he shall gain the whole world, and lose his own soul?"

Behind the power of earthly pressures and spiritual blindness, however, lies a more basic cause: our human nature. There is that in man which makes it easy for him to follow the broad road and miss the narrow way.

The Bible's charge that "all have sinned" flows from the fact that all are sinners. We are "by nature the children of wrath," with a natural mind which is opposed to God and "is not subject to the law of God." Our spiritual state is like an active volcano, from time to time boiling over and erupting, but with the fire always burning inside.

The word "sin" has the letter "i" in the center. The very essence of sin is the placing of ourselves and our desires at the center of our lives, the exaltation of the "I." The prophet Isaiah graphically describes the state of us sinners and the essence of sin in these words: "We have turned every one to his own way."

"The spirit of moral anarchy, suppressed in one area only to break out in another, is as characteristic of man as is the power to feel. You cannot be a man, and not find that again and again evil is occupying the saddle and riding you." [1] In these pointed words Dr. Edwin Lewis has clearly described our basic human problem. The ugly sin of covetousness has taken a firm hold upon our hearts be-

[1] Edwin Lewis, *A Philosophy of the Christian Revelation* (New York: Harper and Brothers, 1940), p. 103.

cause, aside from the grace of God, our fallen human natures find more affinity with getting than giving, love self more than others, and magnify earthly things above heavenly treasures.

III. THE COURSE OF COVETOUSNESS

The prosperous farmer of Jesus' parable furnishes a clear example of the way in which the sin of covetousness often develops. See him as he determines to make just as much as his place will produce. He works long and hard, uses the best methods, practices rigid thrift, and to his joy his harvests are large. In time the place is paid for. Next he is able to buy the adjoining farm and increase his possibility of gain. In addition, he begins to lay by for a rainy day. All of this is accomplished by self-denying thrift and rigid discipline.

You can imagine the neighbors talking to one another about this alert and hard-working young fellow. His qualities of diligence, good management, foresight, and thrift are all commendable. Then we begin to discern the man's basic error. He earned much, but he thought only of himself.

The parable is filled with the first personal pronoun. His aims began and ended in himself. There was no thought for God, who gave fertility to the soil and sent the sunshine and the rain. There was no concern for his fellow men who provided a society in which a man could live and carry on a profitable enterprise. Then, like a thunderclap of doom, came the heavenly voice in judgment: "Thou fool, this night thy soul shall be required of thee: then whose shall those things be, which thou hast provided?"

Often the course of covetousness takes a different direction. "The love of money is the root of all evil" (1 Tim.

6:10), or as it may be translated more accurately, "the root of all kinds of evil." Because of this desire to possess, men and women lie and steal, murder and commit adultery, fight with loved ones and break oaths of office. The daily newspaper furnishes a live commentary on the fruits of covetousness, with a large proportion of reported crime having its beginning in this uncontrolled desire for material gain. The final result of covetousness is uniformly what it was in the case of the farmer in the parable. In the sight of God the man who places material values above spiritual realities is always a fool.

IV. THE CONQUEST OF COVETOUSNESS

The first step in overcoming covetousness is this: let Christ control. Accept him as Saviour and Lord, and earnestly seek to be a faithful and useful Christian. Our fallen human nature furnishes the beachhead from which this sin of covetousness may develop. Our natures need to be changed. We must be born again. By faith in Jesus Christ this miracle of a changed heart, of a spiritual transformation, can become a reality. "Pervasive as greed may be, it is nevertheless a fact that men can have such a sense of the love of God that much of their natural cupidity is purged away. . . . The power of greed is so great that it cannot be handled, in the end, except by a still greater power, the redemptive power of Almighty God."[2] So Dr. Elton Trueblood has declared his faith in the transforming power of God's grace, and so we declare.

"Believe on the Lord Jesus Christ and thou shalt be saved." Through him there is salvation not only from the guilt of sin but from the power of sin—even from the tena-

[2] Elton Trueblood, *Foundations for Reconstruction* (New York: Harper and Brothers, 1946), pp. 106–107.

cious grasp of this terrible sin of covetousness. "If any man be in Christ, he is a new creature: old things are passed away; behold, all things are become new" (2 Cor. 5:17). This is the starting point in our victory over covetousness.

Jesus pointed out another step in overcoming this insidious sin when he warned: "Take heed, and beware of covetousness." In order to be alert against the temptation to covet we must recognize that covetousness is a sin. We must realize how very easy it is to let covetousness take over, and ruin our lives. When his responsibilities crowded on him in such a way that he felt himself slipping spiritually, Henry Grady would sometimes take a train to his old family home and spend an evening with his mother. After praying at her knee as he had done in his boyhood, he returned to his work with a fresh grip upon the matters that count most. So it must be with us in this matter of covetousness—let us be on guard against the very simplest beginning of a covetous spirit.

A further step in the cure of covetousness is the recognition of our position as stewards. As far as other men are concerned, we are owners, but in God's sight we are stewards. It will help us to remember that God is owner of all things—"the cattle upon a thousand hills" and the silver and the gold. It will likewise help us to recall that we have possessions only for a limited time. While we are on earth, they are in our hands; when we leave this life, they pass to other hands. Our privilege is to use whatever may be ours in such a way as to lay up treasures in heaven.

There is nothing about the Christian faith which would forbid a person to become wealthy. Our faith has much to say, however, about the purposes and uses of possessions. We cannot serve both God and mammon, but we can serve God with mammon. Wealth—however large or limited—

can be dedicated to God and will be used by him to do great good.

Liberal giving—with the tithe as the starting point—is an expression of our sense of stewardship and is a powerful antidote for this deadening spirit of covetousness. If we would find a cure for this virus which attacks every one of us, let us keep the springs of liberality flowing, conscious always of our position as stewards of God.

The other suggestion as to the conquering of covetousness is this: live close to God. The writer to the Hebrews, in a luminous statement, points out that the knowledge of God's loving presence gives us such a spiritual fulness that we need not turn to material things for a sense of security: "Let your conversation be without covetousness; and be content with such things as ye have: for he hath said, I will never leave thee, nor forsake thee" (Heb. 13:5).

The habit of prayer is important—regular, sincere, fervent, believing prayer. Remember Jesus' warning: "Watch and pray, that ye enter not into temptation: the spirit indeed is willing, but the flesh is weak" (Matt. 26:41). Constant fellowship with God through the devotional reading of his Word is essential. Since "faith cometh by hearing, and hearing by the word of God," we must keep faith strong by feeding often on this blessed word. In addition, a serious attention to Christlike conduct must mark our lives. After writing to Timothy concerning the dangers of "the love of money," the apostle Paul exhorted the young minister: "But thou, O man of God, flee these things; and follow after righteousness, godliness, faith, love, patience, meekness" (1 Tim. 6:11).

Near the fire the heat is sufficient. When we draw back we are in danger of growing cold. When Peter followed his Lord afar off he fell into deep sin—cowardice, profanity, and denial. So it will be with us. But covetousness can be overcome. Through the power and the presence of the living God the victory will come to those who earnestly trust and obey the living Christ.

When Jesus said, "Take heed, and beware of covetousness," he was talking to you and me. Whether we are rich or poor, well fed or hungry, we are constantly exposed to the danger of letting this desire to possess get out of bounds. We have the example of Jesus, who sought none of this world's goods for himself but gave the world a redeeming message of life and hope. We have the presence of our Lord, always with us through the Holy Spirit, reminding us that "a man's life consisteth not in the abundance of things which he possesseth." We have the power of Christ, leading us from victory unto victory even in the face of our society's strong current of covetousness. Let us beware of covetousness and be strong in the power of the Lord!

The Christian View of Sex

5

MARK 10:6–8
1 CORINTHIANS 6:19–20

J. R. NOFFSINGER

It is easy to understand why preachers seldom preach on the meaning of sex. The pulpit is a sacred trust, and they do not want to risk any misunderstanding in its use. At the same time they recognize sex as one of God's most wonderful gifts. With it God enabled mankind to bring new life into the world. With this gift, God entrusted to each person possibilities for vibrant health and for unity of mind, body, and spirit with another. With it God gave each one those creative forces which can find expression in art and music, literature and poetry, and other lofty fields of human endeavor.

Whenever the pulpit neglects to share God's message regarding the significance of sex, the people are left to seek in secular and often in misguided circles for their understanding of this basic drive of human personality. Of course there are some hazards in a pulpit presentation of this theme. But let us face the fact that even the younger ones in the congregation who would understand the preacher on this subject are far better informed than anyone living in an ivory tower would ever believe. The question is not: *are* they informed, but rather *how* are they informed?

39

Think, too, what impressions are left with both young and old if the pulpit is conspicuously silent on this subject. Are they not likely to come to feel that "good" people just don't talk about such matters? Thus, would we not unwittingly be teaching by our silence the exact opposite of God's will as expressed in his Word?

God created man in his own image, in the image of God created he him; male and female created he them. And God blessed them, and God said unto them, Be fruitful and multiply, and replenish the earth, and subdue it.   GENESIS 1:27–28

For this cause shall a man leave his father and mother, and cleave to his wife; and they twain shall be one flesh: so then they are no more twain, but one flesh.   MARK 10:7–8

I know, and am persuaded by the Lord Jesus, that there is nothing unclean of itself.   ROMANS 14:14

Even though the Christian interpretation of sex has varied through the ages, we are responsible for setting forth its meaning to this generation. As someone has put it: "Let us never be ashamed to speak of that which God was not ashamed to create."

I. SEX IS A PART OF OUR STEWARDSHIP

We are accustomed to think of our stewardship of God's gifts of time, talents, and money. From the creation account in God's Word, however, it is obvious that no entrustment from God to us for our time upon earth was more carefully given than the gift of sex.

God intended that we should so manage this "sweet mystery of life" that our lives should be "fruitful" and that we should "multiply."

This stewardship is so sacred that Jesus often compared himself to the "bridegroom," and those who were to be the "called-out-ones," or the "church," as the "bride." He even stated that "the kingdom of heaven is like unto a certain king, which made a marriage for his son" (Matt. 22:2).

At least from the time of Hosea the relationship of God to his people is pictured as that of marriage, a covenant of "oneness," with the consequences clearly outlined should God's people break so sacred a relationship.

In his letter to the church at Ephesus Paul gives sound counsel on the relation of husband and wife:

Wives, submit yourselves unto your own husbands, as unto the Lord. For the husband is the head of the wife, even as Christ is the head of the church: and he is the saviour of the body. Therefore as the church is subject unto Christ, so let the wives be to their own husbands in every thing. Husbands, love your wives, even as Christ also loved the church, and gave himself for it; that he might sanctify and cleanse it with the washing of water by the word, that he might present it to himself a glorious church, not having spot, or wrinkle, or any such thing; but that it should be holy and without blemish. So ought men to love their wives as their own bodies. He that loveth his wife loveth himself. For no man ever yet hated his own flesh; but nourisheth and cherisheth it, even as the Lord the church: for we are members of his body, of his flesh, and of his bones. For this cause shall a man leave his father and mother, and shall be joined unto his wife, and they two shall be one flesh. This is a great mystery: but I speak concerning Christ and the church. Nevertheless let every one of you in particular so love his wife even as himself; and the wife see that she reverence her husband.   EPHESIANS 5:22–33

This passage leaves no doubt that sex is one of the great gifts which God has entrusted to us with his fullest blessing, to be looked upon as no less holy than the relationship of Christ to his church.

Thus, not only in matters of time, talents and money, but also in matters of sex, "it is required in stewards that a man be found faithful" (2 Cor. 4:2).

II. SEX WAS INTENDED BY GOD FOR "ONENESS"

In the story of creation God said, "It is not good that the man should be alone; I will make an help meet for him."

A professor of pastoral theology wrote concerning the theology of sex and marriage, "There is male who is not complete within himself, and female who is not complete and sufficient within herself. . . . Male and female were not created for separation and isolation but for union and communion. That is, woman was made to complete man and man to complete woman, anatomically, biologically, emotionally, mentally, and spiritually." [1]

According to God's Word, sex was not given to man just as a means to selfish pleasure but as a dynamic unifying force, a means by which the total "oneness" between two children of God could be expressed in tones beyond the range of speech. Those who hold that God intended sex only for the procreation of the race blindly ignore this other basic purpose of God as Jesus re-emphasized it, "that these two shall become one."

We all know that if sex is all two people have in common, physical "oneness" will not suffice. This unity of persons in all their beings—mental, spiritual, and physical—can be expressed through the sex gift. But that sex was intended by God as but a *means* of expressing this unity of two distinct personalities no one can doubt in the light of the biblical revelation.

[1] Revel L. Howe, "A Pastoral Theology of Sex and Marriage," *Pastoral Psychology*, Vol. 3, Sept. 1952, No. 26, p. 37.

III. SEX WAS INTENDED BY GOD FOR PROCREATION

No wonder of life is so awe-inspiring as the wonder shared by a man and a woman responsible for bringing into being a new life.

Who can ever adequately describe the interplay of emotions between mother and father in that moment when they look into the eyes of their newborn child? All realists know that before them wait hours of sleeplessness, that "two o'clock feeding," those back-breaking hours of floor walking with a combination of "sound and fury" known only to a baby with the colic. There wait, the realist knows, the thousands of diaper washings, those endless formulas to fix, those exasperating moments when parents wonder if anyone knows actually how to raise a child, those added responsibilities of "another mouth to feed," and shoes that are outgrown before the last pair has been paid for.

Then there are also those unsettling days ahead when "Jr." comes home with his first black eye and his brand new shirt all torn to shreds, when broken bones and fractured skulls make you wonder how anyone ever grows up "in one piece." There will be those anxious hours when the youth-not-yet-an-adult first starts driving the car, and starts staying out all hours of the night, in love and out of love, until we wonder if our child will ever have a mature love and marriage. Yet, there is no fulfilment in life so precious as the privilege of parenthood with all its terrifying responsibilities.

All this is the creativity of sex. It is a part of our magnificent stewardship which God intended when in the beginning he made humans male and female and commanded them to be fruitful and multiply. The continuation of society upon the earth depends upon human acceptance of sex as God's method of procreation. We must not use this power, therefore, only for our own personal pleasure without regard for God or man. Too much is at stake. It is God's plan that new life can come into being through his mysterious gift of sex.

IV. SEX, FOR THE CHRISTIAN, INVOLVES THE TOTAL PERSONALITY

The Christian gospel gives to every soul a dignity, a value, which can be measured only in the redemptive love of Calvary's cross. All persons are of equal worth in God's sight. Sex becomes a curse rather than a blessing when it is used without regard to the total welfare of the persons involved.

Sexual wrongs are not wrongs simply because some narrow-minded, old-fashioned, puritanical code must not be broken. These wrongs are such because they do injustice to the total needs of a child of God. They are wrong because they serve only the purposes of selfish gratification, not of the mutual fulfilling of two personalities bound together in the holy bonds of marriage.

Children are too precious in the sight of God to become the tragic result of selfishness. Christian love requires of sex that it be used only for the mutual helpfulness of all concerned. It ceases to fulfil its God-intended purpose when used only as a means to selfish pleasure.

"For the Christian, then, sex that is just a mechanical, physical act . . . without any union of spirits is sin. It is false. It is ultimately frustrating. This is what the church would have to say to any of its young people. Anything that treats another person as a mechanism in turn becomes mechanical." [2]

[2] "The Christian Understanding of Sex," a pamphlet published by Whittemore Assoc.

The result of such a relationship will probably be like that in the experience of Tamar and Prince Amnon as recorded in the Old Testament. "The hatred wherewith he hated her was greater than the love wherewith he had loved her." The so-called "love" had not been love after all; it was merely desire—selfish and thoughtless. Once it had been satisfied, despising hatred took its place. This old story truly reflects a tragic possibility of human nature.

The reborn young person or adult who has come under the grace of God unto salvation seeks to do nothing, sexually or otherwise, which will work harm to the physical, mental, emotional, or spiritual welfare of others.

V. SEXUAL SINS CAN BE FORGIVEN AND CORRECTED

The glorious truth of the gospel is that God in Christ forgives, redeems, and reconciles. Many persons carry around with them heavy burdens of guilt concerning sexual matters. Many have had to stumble along, caught up by the tremendous, driving powers of sex and cast down by thoughts and deeds which have left emotional and spiritual scars never really faced and dealt with. In our pride we hate to reveal our innermost problems. Feeling shame, too many of us rarely seek help from others, even when we know they could help. Some feel that God just "won't forgive *my* sins."

Yet more than once when Jesus confronted such a sinner, what did he do? Condemn? No, for he came not to condemn but to save. In the home of a Pharisee, a woman came to Jesus and bathed his feet with her tears. The Pharisees scorned him again as they said, "This man, if he were a prophet, would have known who and what manner of woman this is that toucheth him: for she is a sinner." But Jesus replied, "Her sins, which are many, are forgiven" (Luke 7:47).

How desperately do some need to throw aside pride and face their problems honestly and frankly with those who are competent to help them! How all of us need to know God's forgiveness and to learn his will for us in our management of his gift of sex! No problem is too great for him to solve, or to be met victoriously when matched with his grace. Pastors and other personal counselors who share the innermost problems of folk can testify again and again to the marvelous release from fear and guilt which such honest facing of such problems, coupled with the redeeming grace of God, can bring.

One of the most helpful writers in this field has said:

The Biblical concept of sex life contains a blessed and liberating element, for it gives us courage to reassert that sex is a precious thing in spite of the sins which are connected with it. By faith, however, sex life becomes different from what it was. It is transferred into a higher relation; it ceases to be merely a matter of a purely natural character. Rather it is seen as something which serves the divine purpose. This fact confers nobility and value upon it; but again this same fact makes the transgression of its inner order a burden that weighs on our life, endangering and destroying life's very meaning.[3]

Multitudes know most of what they need to know about sex, but they have never learned God's way to let this power fulfil its intended purposes. Others have never had the guidance they need. Parents are often timid, schools often silent, and pulpits often evasive so that God's great gift of sex brings heartache and shame rather than the blessings he intended. If you have such problems, by God's grace, find those who can help you know God's way to manage his gift of sex.

[3] Otto A. Piper, *The Christian Interpretation of Sex*, Charles Scribner's Sons, 1941, p. 187.

For truly, "sexual experience can mean only what two persons bring to it. It can be the release of psycho-biological tension with no regard for the other person involved, or it can be a means of expressing in joyous outgoing concern that sense of community which one would renew with his beloved, with his fellowman, and with God." [4]

When you have reached this understanding, you can "glorify God in your body, and in your spirit, which are God's" (1 Cor. 6:20).

[4] Peter A. Bertocci, "Toward A Christian View of Sex Education," *Pastoral Psychology.* Vol. 4. February 1953. No. 31, pp. 53, 54.

Christian Love and Marriage

6

THEODORE F. ADAMS

Newspaper readers in St. Louis were startled recently when they opened up the *St. Louis Post Dispatch* and found a paid advertisement in which a man paid a tribute to his wife and said he wanted to thank her publicly for giving him the twenty-one nicest years of his life. Reporters hurried out to his home to find out what this was all about. Why in the world would a man buy space in the newspapers to tell the world and his wife how happy he was?

He told them he had been so disturbed by reading in the newspapers about all the unhappiness in marriage, the divorces, and the problems of married couples that somebody should advertise the fact that he was happily married and wanted the world to know it. The reporters discovered that he was in truth a very happy man. He told them that he gave God all the credit for the happiness he and his wife had known in marriage, stating that any man who is missing the spiritual side of life is missing its most important aspect. He was frankly surprised that so many people thought his action unusual because he said, "There must be thousands of happy people like us," and there are!

It is so easy to lose sight of the fact that there are thousands of happily married couples who are overcoming the tensions of life together and are finding the joys that life and love can bring. But they do not buy space in the news-papers to say so. On the other hand, you know that there are many couples that are divorced—a thousand divorces a day is our national record—and many other homes where a veneer of respectability covers inward tragedy or suffering.

Bishop Donavan at the Cathedral of St. John in New York spoke about the importance of Christian homes the day the Queen Mother from England unveiled the "Motherhood Window" in the great cathedral. The bishop said that we had better read the handwriting on the wall before our civilization goes the way of others. The spiritual health and welfare of the community, the nation, and the world depend, not on scientific progress or material achievements, but on the stability of the home, which is the basic unit of our human society. A united, harmonious Christian home is the purifying influence on society which prevents the world from going bad. Whereas the divorce rate across the country got as low as one divorce for every 3.1 marriages, among Christian marriages, both partners active in the same church, it is only one divorce in about fifty marriages.

How can those troubled homes be avoided? How can we find the kind of life and love God meant his children to know? The answer largely depends on what you mean by love. In the Christian concept of marital love you will find the way to success and happiness in marriage. It is strange but true that you may be "in love" with someone that you cannot happily and successfully marry. Love is essential, but love is not enough.

Some will say, "Oh, we love each other and everything will work out all right. Love will find a way." They have a lot to learn about marriage and about life. It is entirely possible for you to love someone very deeply and sincerely and yet face the fact that happy marriage is not possible for you and that person. Sometimes this is because the other person does not love you, and sometimes because you just are not made for each other.

Sometimes people only imagine they are in love. They may be having a very delightful experience. They are just in love with love and with the delights and pleasures which such an infatuation can bring. They may have a lovely time, but it is not the kind of love that can lead to happy marriage. There are all kinds of love, as you know, paternal and parental, maternal and fraternal. Marital love, however, draws together one man and one woman to make a solemn promise to forsake all others and keep only to each other so long as they both shall live. That "mate" love has some qualities of its own. It has strength and vitality, backbone and dynamic. So let us ask some penetrating questions that will help to evaluate true marital love.

1. Are you always patient with the one you love? Do you put his or her needs and wants before your own? Do you long to be together but have other common interests in addition to physical attraction?

2. Do you look for the good qualities in the one you love and dwell on them and try to help him or her overcome failings and shortcomings by gentle suggestions and loving understanding?

3. Do you refuse to be jealous when the one you love fails to give you his undivided attention at all times?

4. Do you love this person for what he really is, rather than for who he is, how he rates in the community, or what material success he has achieved?

5. Do you treat the one you love with the same cour-

tesy and thoughtfulness you display toward strangers and business acquaintances?

6. Are you glad to see the one you love receive the main credit and spotlight for accomplishments in which you have had a part?

7. Does your love protect you from being easily hurt or provoked by little thoughtless things the other does?

8. Has your love endured even after you have discovered unpleasant traits or even wrong-doing in the object of your affections?

9. Do you have complete faith and trust in the one you love, never holding anything back, never resorting to half-truths?

10. Do you have many common interests and things you like to do together?

11. Are you really proud of this partner, with nothing to be ashamed of or to apologize for?

12. Do you have a strong desire to please him or her, even if it means giving up your own preference?

13. Can you disagree without being disagreeable, and still love and respect each other?

14. Do troubles and crises push you apart or draw you together?

Those questions are a good test of marital love—the kind of love you need if you are going to make a success of your marriage. Such a love is at its best when it has a Christian basis. If you want happiness in marriage, you need a Christian concept of marital love.

Just as life has many tests so love as Christians see it has many bonds, and while no single strand can bear the strain, the many strands bound together can withstand every test. The Christian concept of marital love recognizes that that love must have a *physical* basis. You want to be with the one you love, to possess and be possessed, recognizing the sacredness of all the physical relationships of marriage. There is also an *emotional* bond in love, a bond that draws you together and helps you to face crises and sorrows when they come. This emotional element in love provides the power within that makes it possible to do things that you never could or would do, but for love.

There is also a *mental* bond in love. Common interests and ideals and similar backgrounds and hopes are of great significance. That is, two people in love should have matching minds as well as a physical desire for each other. The Christian concept of marital love stresses the importance of the *spiritual* bond of union. Christian love has certain qualities that every marriage needs for living above the merely respectable plane.

Paul gives some of love's essential elements in 1 Corinthians 13: "Love is patient, kind. It has no jealousies. It is never rude, never selfish, never resentful, never irritating, is gladdened by goodness, always desires the best." Phillips translates it this way:

This love of which I speak is slow to lose patience—it looks for a way of being constructive. It is not possessive: it is neither anxious to impress, nor does it cherish inflated ideas of its own importance.

Love has good manners and does not pursue selfish advantage. It is not touchy. It does not compile statistics of evil nor gloat over the wickedness of other people. On the contrary, it is glad with all good men when truth prevails.

Love knows no limit to its endurance, no end to its trust, no fading of its hope: it can outlast anything.

If you let that kind of love grow in your heart and nurture it through worship and prayer, you will find that your love will be sufficient for any tests that life can bring.

Fortunately, that kind of love does grow. Not long ago I talked with a father who had been desperately concerned about his son. He said, "You know, when he fell in love with that Christian girl, you never would have believed the difference it made in his life. She has brought out his best and has strengthened him where he was weak. His love has grown to match hers, and his life to match hers." The same miracle can happen over and over again to those who say to the Lord Christ, "You are the Lord of love. Come in and take over my life and help me to be worthy of the one I love and to grow a love that will meet every test of life."

One of the greatest souls of the last century sums it all up in a prayer. To me it is one of the finest prayers for lovers that I have ever seen. It was a prayer written for the wedding of someone that he loved. "Invoke Thy gentlest blessing on all who love. We pray Thee for the great longing that draws the soul of man and woman together and bids them leave all the bonds of the past to cleave to one another. We thank Thee for the revealing power of love which divines in the one beloved the mystic beauty and glory of humanity. We thank Thee for the transfiguring power of love which ripens and ennobles our nature, calling forth the hidden stores of tenderness and strength and overcoming the selfishness of youth by the passions of self-surrender. We pray Thee to make love strong, holy and deathless, that no misunderstandings may fray the bonds and no grey disenchantment of the years may have power to quench the heavenly light that glows within. May they early gain wisdom to discern the true values of life and may no tyranny of passion, no glamour of cheaper joys filch from them the wholesome peace and inner satisfaction that only love can give. Grant them sober eyes to look beyond the sweet days of friendship to the generations yet to come and to realize that the home for which they long will be part of the sacred tissue of the body of humanity in which Thou art to dwell, so that they may reverence themselves and drink love's cup of joy with awe." [1]

That is Christian love at its finest and its best. Those who cherish that ideal and ask the help of the Lord Christ to live up to it will find that kind of love can be theirs. Perhaps you feel like a girl who once said to me, "Dr. Adams, I thank you for your sermon. All I need is two things—the man and ten years to get ready." Well, the man will come in God's good time, and perhaps it won't take ten years to get ready. It is wonderful how love in the heart of one can nurture love and growth in another.

Or you may say, "Dr. Adams, you put the standard very high." Of course, I do. I could not say that you should settle for something less than the best in love, or marry anybody who just happens to come along. To be sure, we do present a *Christian* ideal for love and marriage and hold the standard high. As you do, too, you will find that others will rise with you.

There are certain qualities you need to seek in a mate, and which you should cultivate in yourself, both before and after marriage. You can sum them up in four C's. The first is to *be a Christian* and to live like a Christian. The personal Christian virtues ought to be in evidence not only in the one you love but in your own life as well. The second vital quality is *character*. Such basic characteristics as honesty, integrity, and righteousness are essential. Many a home crumbles because the foundation is weakened by dishonesty or some other sin or bad habit. When the foundation is weak the home is likely to fall.

[1] Walter Rauschenbusch.

Christian character is essential and with it a third element ranks high, *consideration*. You need to ask, "How does she treat other people? How does she treat her own people?" That is the way *you* will be treated, too. Quite often someone will come to me, troubled about a future mate, because he or she is so inconsiderate, often doing or saying thoughtless things that hurt. You run a risk when you marry a person like that. Courtship and engagement should bring out the best in people. Take plenty of time to be sure you really know the one you are to marry for this quality of consideration is very important.

The fourth "C" calls for *consecration*. You want a life partner who is constant and dependable, one who is true to you and determined with your help and God's to make your marriage succeed.

If your marriage is to succeed, you need to take your time about it. Take time in courtship. Don't rush or be rushed into marriage. Take time for a happy and worthwhile period of growth and comradeship after your engagement is announced. If your marriage is going to get off to the right start, there are certain things you need to talk about and settle before you marry.

Then it is tremendously important that the co-operative nature of marriage be understood from the beginning. Whenever you go to the little Church in the Wildwood, the guide will show you the bell near the front door. It figures in an interesting custom after each wedding there. The minister walks with the bride and the groom to the door and says to the bride, "It is time for the wedding bells to ring; here is the rope—we'll let you ring the bell." She tries in vain to pull the heavy rope. Then the minister says to the groom, "You take hold of the rope with her and both of you pull." And when the wedding bells ring out, the minister says, "Marriage is just like the bell; it works far better if you pull together."

Of course you ought to know about the mental and the physical health of the one you marry and of the family from which he or she comes. You ought to have frank talks about money—no matter how much or how little it is going to be. Who is going to earn it? Who is going to spend it, and how it is going to be spent. Talk it over together and draw up a budget for yourselves. You ought to talk about children—whether you both want children, how many, and whether they are to come soon or be delayed. Discuss frankly all of the factors you can with reference to sex. Before you are married, see your doctor and have a good physical checkup. Talk to him about your marriage and your physical relationships.

The wedding itself is of genuine importance. Have you ever asked yourself why people cry at weddings? The cynic would say that people cry because they feel sorry for the two young folks who don't know what they are getting into. There are some who are moved emotionally by the sheer beauty of it all. There are some who weep tears of joy and gratitude; joy, for they know what love at its best can mean to the two that are pledging life and love to each other; gratitude, because it is possible for these two under such lovely auspices to start a Christian home together. Yes, there are a good number of reasons why people cry—there are tears of bitterness and there are tears of joy.

By all means, talk with your pastor about the wedding and also about your future church relationship. You will find he can help you in many ways. Plan a wedding in keeping with your circumstances, with a sacred and memorable service.

Following the wedding there is a honeymoon that gives you time to start learning how to live together, to get over the strain and stress of the wedding, and to start with a sense of oneness that will grow through the years. It is important, of course, to keep the sense of romance all through your marriage.

Problems sometimes arise in marriage because the couple think that what they knew as romance before marriage constitutes romance after marriage. But marriage calls for a different type of romance, for a deeper love and new expressions of it. If you think that romance in marriage is just a continuation of your courtship experiences and that is all that will satisfy, then you are taking an immature view both of love and marriage. With such a concept you can never know the best that marriage can bring, because you still cherish an adolescent concept of what love and romance can be. If you will nurture your love and romance and expect it to grow and mature, you will find that life grows richer and more beautiful as the days go by. The promises of your early love will be fulfilled in ways of which you never dreamed, and life will be far better than you had ever dared to hope.

An older man who has learned that Christian love can grow with the years gave me something he had written not long ago. He said, "I have written it out of my years of experience." In writing it, he paid a lovely tribute, all unconsciously, both to his wife and to himself. Speaking about the happiness he had known in marriage, he said, "It is no secret at all. It is just common sense. Anyone can do it. I have pledged myself to love and care for her in sickness and in good health, so long as we both live. Immediately after the wedding I started out learning how to keep my promise. I was determined to do everything in my power to make her happy, and it wasn't long before I discovered that she was doing everything in her power to make me happy, and so our cares became one, and I learned always that when I was doing something to please her, she was trying her best to do something to please me."

It is just as simple as that for that is what Christian love does. Love seeketh not its own. It is always patient, always kind, always eager to believe the best and give the best. Such a love never disappears, but grows in beauty and in promise through the years.

The Christian Attitude Toward Divorce

7

MATTHEW 19:1–12

SCOTT L. TATUM

One day I answered a knock on the door and invited into my study John and Mary, one of the finest young couples in our church. They joined in relating a story which came as a complete surprise to me. Before either of them became Christians, they had engaged in general immorality, and when John was a teenager, he and a girl friend had run away to get married. Their marriage, built on almost no foundation, soon failed and divorce followed. Some time later John met Mary; they were married, had children, and were converted. I had baptized them. Now they said, "We've been reading our Bibles, and while we love each other dearly, we are willing to dissolve our home and give each other up if we are living in adultery in the sight of God."

Their case, involving many other problems, was far too complex to be solved by any one all inclusive rule or law. They had to let God find them where they were and lead them as close to his standard as was possible in view of their past lives.

My dealing with them, to summarize briefly, involved pointing out that they would have to learn to live with themselves under conditions already blighted by guilt for past foolishness and sin and to let God help them to overcome their guilt by his grace. Breaking up another home with so many possibilities for use by the Lord was certainly not the solution.

Another pastor relates the case of a young woman who had unknowingly married a sexual pervert and who after months of misery divorced him. She said to her pastor, "I am a very lonely person, and if I find the right person, I should like to marry again. Does the Bible force me to remain single the remainder of my life?"

I do not know how that pastor answered her, but if I understand the spirit and the principles of Jesus, I am sure the Master would have been as sympathetic toward one sinned against in the matter of perversion as one sinned against in adultery. To say the least, God had to find that young woman where she was and help her to be as much like his standard as possible under the circumstances.

In dealing with human beings, God always takes them where they are, and if they will receive his help, he will lead them step by step toward his perfect standard. As Christians we must often counsel with those who have already become involved in marital tensions or even divorce. It is not ours to excuse or gloss over the past. They need help where they are that they might become more useful to society, happier with themselves, and at peace with God.

I. GOD'S PERFECT STANDARD

Let us look briefly at God's perfect standard, and let us help those who, according to Matthew 19:12, are "able to receive it" to keep their lives free from all things that might cause them to have to live under "second best" conditions. Those whose lives are yet unblighted by marital problems, especially young people, should recognize that anything less than God's standard will make life full of unhappiness, guilt, complex problems, and a usefulness for God limited by the time and energy consumed in dealing with these problems.

God's standard was set forth in creation in that he made one man for one woman for life. In Genesis 2:24 we read, "Therefore shall a man leave his father and his mother, and shall cleave unto his wife: and they shall be one flesh." After quoting from Genesis, Jesus said, "Wherefore they are no more twain, but one flesh. What therefore God hath joined together, let not man put asunder" (Matt. 19:6).

Marriage is a matter so important to society and to the kingdom of God as to demand special attention in the training of our youth. Marriage is seldom better than it is planned for. Training should include the idea that Christian marriage is a covenant like that existing between the Saviour and his saved people. That is exactly the illustration Paul used in Ephesians 5.

Because the covenant of marriage is so sacred in the sight of God, it follows that God's will may be found for each individual in marriage. I believe no person should marry without the conviction found in prayer that the step is according to the will of God. This idea alone would save a multitude from unfortunate relationships which only by the stretch of terminology could be called marriage. A contract entered into without the leadership of the Spirit of God is almost surely destined for failure, and only by the grace of God can become to a degree satisfactory. And within the standard of God's will for marriage, that one man and one woman who have made a lifetime covenant must realize that their marriage is something for them to build.

Evelyn Millis Duvall in *Building Your Marriage* (a Public Affairs Pamphlet) related the story of a young couple who had to learn that a happy marriage does not just happen. It must be built.

Jerry and Ethel were married just before Jerry went overseas. They had known each other a long while and had been planning on getting married even before the war. But they had just six weeks together before Jerry had to leave. When they were finally reunited they found that although they had been married nearly three years, actually they had many adjustments to make that are common to newlyweds. They had to work out their money affairs from scratch. They had to decide whether Ethel would continue to work, who would pay the bills, what they would buy, how much they could save, and make many other important everyday decisions. Each had to learn to respond to the other, to talk freely, to listen, to get through to each other, even to love each other as fully as each desired. Friends and fun and family and fights loomed so large as adjustment areas at times that Jerry and Ethel each secretly feared their marriage might be classified 4F. Yet theirs was potentially a good marriage. It only needed building.

God's perfect standard then is one man and one woman building a home together as a lifetime experience for God.

II. THE DIVORCE PROBLEM

But over against this perfect standard of God there is the tremendously complex divorce problem, and the larger problem of which it is only a part—the problem of the broken home. In 1870 the ratio of divorces to marriages was one to thirty-four. In 1890 it was one to sixteen. In 1910 it was one to eleven. In 1920 it was one to six. In 1940 it was one to five. In 1950 it was one to three. On my desk I have a letter from the judge of the family court in a

Louisiana city telling me that for the first six months of 1955 there were 349 legal separations and divorces in his parish and 522 marriage licenses issued. That trend, if long continued, will mean that over half of the marriages will end in divorce. We ought to be much more alarmed than we are. The very fact that society is not unusually concerned is evidence of moral decay. We have too readily accepted a standard far below God's standard.

In all fairness it must be stated here that comparing the number of divorces to the number of marriages in any one year or any one place might be quite misleading inasmuch as the divorces are usually marriage failures from previous years and often involve people who have moved from one section of the country to another. It is also true that many divorce suits are filed in court which are not finally granted. The records are usually taken from the number of suits filed. At any rate, the condition is alarming.

The by-products of divorce are often as tragic as divorce itself. For every broken home there are at least two unhappy people plagued to some extent by guilt and shame. Often there are children destined to insecurity which may cause serious personality damage and eventual marital unhappiness when they attempt to build a home of their own. Society frequently pays an additional cost for juvenile delinquency, court costs, aid to dependent children, etc. According to the annual report of the Louisiana Department of Institutions released on October 17, 1955, the following predictions were presented: "If you live in Louisiana and are divorced, the odds of going to a State Mental Hospital are seven times greater than if you are married, and chances are thirty times more that your children will wind up in a State Correction School."

But despite all that is bad about divorce, we must also

admit that there are homes in which men and women have not violated God's commandment as to overt adultery, but have committed in their hearts so many infidelities that life has withered away into one horrible, armed truce which cannot by any stretch of the imagination be called a marriage.

Notice some of the major causes of marital friction that often lead to broken homes and divorce. No longer are homes isolated units with husband and wife mutually dependent as in the old-time one-family farm home. Ours is a complex civilization in which husbands and wives are often financially independent. Much of modern society no longer looks on divorce as evidence of marital failure. Sometimes divorce is even glamorized as in such phrases as "the gay divorcee."

Misunderstanding as to the meaning of marriage sometimes leads to unhappiness in the home. The husband may expect his wife always to be the movie type "glamor girl," or the wife expects her husband to be her "dream man," only to awaken ultimately to the realization that marriage usually involves two average people who must learn to work out their problems together.

Widely conflicting interests on the part of husband and wife usually indicate a lack of preparation for marriage or a failure to work together after marriage. Although this condition is often a cause of divorce, it need not be. Those interests can be brought together through loyalty to Christ.

Twisted ideas of sex constitute one of the more dangerous threats to the existence of the home. Perversion, adultery, homosexuality, and similar problems should have the careful attention of trained physicians. Sometimes the conditions are so abnormal as to make marriage impossible. It is at this point that Jesus did at least allow divorce.

God does not expect a human personality to live in an animalistic sexual situation. Repentance, regeneration, and forgiveness are, of course, the ideal solution, but often because of the unwillingness of one or the other party this is impossible.

Alcohol has been called the greatest enemy of the home. In one juvenile court alcohol was involved in at least 75 per cent of the cases. It is probably involved in that many, or more, of the divorce cases that come before our courts. This enemy must be attacked not only by regeneration, but also by education and legislation.

While we cannot mention all of the causes for divorce, certainly we cannot overlook problems with "in-laws" and problems about money. Real Christians must work these problems out in a spirit of Christian forbearance and patience, realizing that marriage is a give and take proposition.

Mixed marriages and homes with no religion cannot be ignored as contributing to the rate of divorce. In a recent Public Affairs Pamphlet the following statistics were reported. Among Jewish homes 4.6 per cent are broken; among Catholics 6.4 per cent; among Protestants 6.8 per cent. Among mixed families of Catholics and Protestants 15.2 per cent are broken homes, and in homes where neither partner is a church member 16.7 per cent are broken. Being members of the same church helps a couple succeed in marriage; being consecrated Christians brings power to meet life's keenest problems and find happiness at the same time.

III. FACING THE ISSUES

As all these problems confront the home, is divorce ever justified? Jesus declared that divorce is permissible only on grounds of sexual immorality, but even then if repentance and forgiveness can be found that is a better way. Jesus permitted divorce. He did not advise or command it. The story of Hosea is a classic illustration of the power of love over sin. God's willingness to take back the adulterous nation of Israel as his own bride is another illustration.

Moses found himself in a society where men were divorcing their wives for almost any reason. God led him to help the people to make as much advance as possible by instituting the "written bill of divorcement." This limited and regulated the vice, but Jesus said this was never God's perfect will. It was the best God could do with a rebellious people. Unfortunately today, because of sin, the best God can do with his children is all too often far from his ideal standard.

Is remarriage ever permissible after divorce? Matthew 5 and Matthew 19 both seem to imply that it is, and in Jewish history there was always the idea of remarriage involved in divorce. "And when she is departed out of his house, she may go and be another man's wife" (Deut. 24:2). That is why Jesus said to divorce an innocent woman was to make her appear in the eyes of society an adulteress and leave her exposed to a world in which immorality was almost inevitable. Inasmuch as Jesus did not recognize divorce except for sexual immorality and presumed that divorce reflected it, he said, "Whoso marrieth her which is put away doth commit adultery."

What about the person who has already been touched by the problem of divorce? God must find him or her where he is, and he must let God guide him to be as nearly like his divine pattern as he can be now under the circumstances. There may be wounds easily healed and again there may be scars that the divorced person must bear to the grave. As God dealt with ancient Israel, as

Hosea dealt with Gomer, and as Christ dealt with the woman at the well, God can deal with a divorced man or woman and give him or her a place of service, humble though it may be.

Jesus our Saviour died on the cross to save from all sin and to redeem lives from all circumstances. He said, "I am come that they might have life, and that they might have it more abundantly." God still calls: "Come now, and let us reason together, saith the Lord: though your sins be as scarlet, they shall be as white as snow; though they be red like crimson, they shall be as wool."

In divorce, as in every other problem, of course, an ounce of prevention is worth a pound of cure. We must train our boys and girls from childhood to youth to be prepared for Christian marriage. We must pray for and counsel with couples who are having problems, and we must be sympathetic and helpful to those whose lives need to be redeemed.

Public Enemy Number One ‖8

PROVERBS 20:1

W. R. WHITE

Intoxicants make men superficial and cynical. Under the influence of alcohol men often reject, flaunt, and deride the most precious realities of life. Frequently men who drink become boisterous, uncouth troublemakers. In fact, too often otherwise decent human beings become bestial and brutal under the influence of beverage alcohol.

In the Bible, distilled liquors were unknown. The common drink was wine. There was the fresh juice of the vine, slightly fermented wine, and the highly fermented drink.

The use of intoxicants as a beverage is strongly condemned in the Bible. Concerning it, woes and warnings are frequently pronounced.

Woe unto them that rise up early in the morning, that they may follow strong drink; that continue until night, till wine inflame them!

Woe unto them that are mighty to drink wine, and men of strength to mingle strong drink: which justify the wicked for reward, and take away the righteousness of the righteous from him! ISAIAH 5:11, 22–23

Who hath woe? who hath sorrow? who hath contentions? who hath babbling? who hath redness of eyes?

They that tarry long at the wine; they that go to seek mixed wine.

68

Look not thou upon the wine when it is red, when it giveth his colour in the cup, when it moveth itself aright.

Thine eyes shall behold strange women, and thine heart shall utter perverse things. PROVERBS 23:29–31, 33

Sometimes its medical use is commended. Paul's advice to Timothy is familiar: "Drink no longer water, but use a little wine for thy stomach's sake and thine often infirmities" (1 Tim. 5:23). At other times wine is referred to as a symbol of prosperity and joy.

The over-all, general trend of the whole Bible, however, must be the rule for determining its teachings. Its paramount, profound principles must not be set aside by a few difficult passages. This is not only true of intoxicants, but is applicable to all other issues as well. And the general teaching of the Bible concerning the dangers involved in using alcoholic beverages is crystal clear.

I. THE ENEMY OF LIFE

Beverage alcohol kills many more people than knives, guns, and poisonous drugs each year. It is like a cocked pistol on the highways. A driver under the influence of alcohol (he does not have to be drunk) has his reflexes slowed down and his co-ordination so confused as to be a constant menace—a potential killer. Scatter these along the highways of America, and you have a danger equal to firing a bank of artillery at random. In the country as a whole, from 25 to 50 per cent of the highway accidents and deaths are attributed by many to beverage alcohol.

Beverage alcohol is a great enemy of personal and public health. It makes thousands more susceptible to certain diseases—and in their most dangerous forms. It weakens resistance and undermines recuperative powers. Some insurance companies take these facts into consideration and give lower rates to total abstainers.

Alcoholics are becoming so numerous as to be a national problem. They practically disappeared in the early years of prohibition when there was a decent effort to enforce the laws. They began to appear again when defiance of the dry laws became widespread. The return of legal liquor has greatly accelerated the increase of drunkards—alcoholics—helpless human wrecks who have lost control of when they drink and how much they drink. Authorities estimate that there are now in the United States 4,000,000 alcoholics with an additional 3,000,000 habitual heavy drinkers. This so-called disease ranks along with tuberculosis and cancer as a public health problem.

No slavery is more galling and no mental torture more wretched than that endured by the unfortunate victims of liquor's horrible power. There is no preventive and no permanent cure without total abstinence. No one who drinks can be *sure* that he will not become an alcoholic, and no alcoholic can take one drink without being thrown back into the miserable cycle again. It is the only disease that society seeks to cure without making the primary attack on the cause. In fact, society sanctions, legalizes, and nurtures the cause.

II. IT IS AN ENEMY OF THE HOME

No one thing produces as much domestic misery, unhappiness, and instability as beverage alcohol. It sends an unending stream to the court room. It feeds the divorce mill as no other factor does. Evangeline Booth well said:

> DRINK has drained more blood,
> Hung more crepe,

Sold more homes,
Plunged more people into bankruptcy,
Armed more villains,
Slain more children,
Snapped more wedding rings,
Defiled more innocence,
Blinded more eyes,
Twisted more limbs,
Dethroned more reason,
Wrecked more manhood,
Dishonored more womanhood,
Broken more hearts,
Blasted more lives,
Driven more to suicide,
And dug more graves
    Than any other poisoned scourge
    that ever swept its death-dealing
    waves across the world.

It frequently disqualifies the parents for rearing children. This is beginning to apply to the mother as well as to the father to an alarming degree. Domestic strife, discord, confusion, and irresponsibility are becoming the order of the day. Liquor is the big factor in it all. Alcoholism ranks almost on a par with adultery, desertion, and cruelty as grounds for divorce.

In Cook County, Illinois, a special research study showed that the divorce rate among alcoholics was almost six times as great as that of the general population. "Six out of every ten juvenile delinquents have fathers who drink to excess; many have mothers who drink to excess, according to Doctors Sheldon and Eleanor Glueck, husband and wife sociology team who were called before a Congressional inquiry probing juvenile delinquency."

III. AN ENEMY OF SOCIETY

Liquor frequently makes its users lawless and even dangerous. It is continuously breaking out in antisocial acts. It requires extravagantly expensive surveillance. Otherwise, it would produce an impossible situation for law and order. Law enforcement officers could be reduced in number and could be paid better salaries were it not for beverage alcohol.

Those who sell liquor, in the main, have a tendency to subvert the law and corrupt politics. Court records proving the bad citizenship of liquor dealers if compiled would fill the Library of Congress. It is a sordid trail from the beginning of our country's history until the present moment. No business has to bout so many curbs and regulations as the business of beverage alcohol. It requires eternal, costly vigilance.

Its antisocial nature is revealed by the company it keeps. Prostitution and gambling follow it. Crime-breeding night spots would go out of business without beverage alcohol. The sexually stimulating dance and general immorality flourish where liquor is plentiful.

The high-powered, intricate machinery of the industrial world and mechanized military weapons can be rendered useless by alcoholic operators. Well-focused eyes, clear mind, and steady nerves are needed, and liquor is a bitter foe to each. Every civilization has been pickled in alcohol sooner or later. Ours is following the same pattern except with greater speed due to our machinery.

IV. IT IS THE ENEMY OF SPIRITUAL VALUES

"Dearly beloved, I beseech you as strangers and pilgrims, abstain from fleshly lusts, which war against the soul," wrote Peter to first-century Christians, and his counsel is still pertinent to our own sensate culture.

The body is the temple of the Holy Spirit. It should not be poisoned but kept clean. It should not be filled with strong drink but should be stimulated by the Spirit from which comes melody and good will. Those who are excited with a false sense of exhilaration will have a real letdown. Alcohol is a stimulant which is habit forming. It carries its own inherent demand for repetition; one drink calls for another one. Its thrill weakens with the habit-forming process, requiring more and more to bring the stimulation up to the same point of excitement. Being filled with the Spirit brings similar but superior exuberance with no effects of dissipation. Beverage alcohol creates a fool's paradise of "make believe." The Holy Spirit engenders a real paradise in which there is no disillusionment. "Be not drunk with wine, wherein is excess; but be filled with the Spirit; speaking to yourselves in psalms and hymns and spiritual songs, singing and making melody in your heart to the Lord" (Eph. 5:18–19).

On a train coming out of New Orleans a conductor once asked another minister and me to witness an unforgettable sight. A drunken woman was sprawled in the doorway of the women's restroom with the odorous remnants of her previous meal soiling her face and clothes. She was unconscious. Her purse had fallen to the floor open. The contents were spilled in all directions. Her hair was disheveled and mixed up with the whole conglomeration. It was revolting—tragic—disgusting.

The other minister and I witnessed the counting of the money in and out of her purse. Then we helped to carry her limp body to her berth. At this point a problem arose. She had been able to get only an upper. A lovely woman who had the lower beneath her gladly exchanged berths with her.

Next morning she was sober. After a complete work-over in the restroom, she came out looking quite respectable, neat, and trim. What a contrast to the wreck of the evening before! Seeing the charming husband meet her, but still with the picture of the night before in my mind, I could only loathe and hate the damnable stuff that would make a repulsive beast out of an otherwise attractive human being.

This kind of scene makes a Christian understand the deeper meaning of Paul's conviction: "It is good neither to eat flesh, nor to drink wine, nor any thing whereby thy brother stumbleth, or is offended, or is made weak" (Rom. 14:21).

Several years ago I witnessed the salvation and rehabilitation of a pathetic wreck. For twenty years he had been a temperate drinker who could "take it or leave it alone"— he said. But financial worries made him more and more dependent on alcohol. He became an alcoholic.

His family endured it as long as they could. Finally, he lost his business. He secured a good job and then lost it. It was a heartbreaking situation. Many were praying for him.

One day while he was on his way to Dallas, he passed through a small town and felt an irresistible urge to get some whiskey. But soon after he turned his car toward his favorite place in this community, he was seized by weakness and cold chills. When he turned back toward the highway, a normal feeling returned rapidly. The gnawing appetite, however, continued to possess him. Three times he tried to go for his liquor, but each time a restraining power laid hold on him, with the same weakening, chilling sensation.

He went back to his room, got out his dust-covered Bible. He read. He called on the Saviour. He was gloriously saved from his sins and liberated from his enslaving appetite.

I saw him come back into full possession of his faculties and of his manhood. He was able to convince his family of his sincerity. His home was restored. He was given a new chance in business and regained the respect of the community. This he did not betray. It was wonderful to behold.

Decency and liquor have nothing in common. Some people may be decent in spite of it, but nobody is made better because of it.

LUKE 3:8-9

CARLYLE MARNEY

John the Baptist never was a very complacent sort of preacher. Out of the Palestinian wilderness, perhaps from a little community of hardly-known Essenes, came this wild sort of fellow, and he got a hearing. Eternal voices frequently come from wilderness places, and sometimes such voices are heard by people who are not wild at all.

As a matter of fact, John's hearers were a *religious* people. They comprised the largest population group within their nation. They enrolled the most respected elements of their culture. They were a participating group in the respected institutional religion of their day. Their salvation was being constantly reassured to them by annual blood atonement. They were favored in their own eyes, and in God's—especially blessed, picked, chosen. How often had they heard preached the doctrine of their own chosen-ness! Like our own "eternal security of the believer," it had become common property of the layman on the street: we are God's own!

The reality of their personal religion, however, like ours, was another matter. In the main it consisted of attendance upon the public functions, reasonable observance of custom and law, enjoyment of traditional assurances, with a grand seasonal series of revival as diversion. It was upon

76

a people much like us that this wilderness bomber burst with his strange doctrine that when people have repented they ought to give evidence of it. No wonder they listened. So John preached, in the wilderness towns, and his words fell like hot shrapnel at the first. Repent! Who? Me?

The thing that jarred even Jerusalem in John's preaching was his flat denial of their indispensableness. Their pet doctrine said: *"Chosen!"* John said: *"God does not have to use you!* There is no most-favored nation with God. He is able of these stones to raise up his needs." And God did. In less than twenty years he was raising men to do his will from stones—Gentile rubble off the hills of Southeast Europe.

He raised us up from rubble; to these chosen, satisfied Jews, our ancestors were but stones. And now, we have replaced the Jews as God's chosen ones—strange it sounds to our ears that God does not have to have us. Repent! Who, me? And for what?

There are moments in history, moments in the life of races, of nations, of cultures, and of churches, which, if seized, lead to immortality; or, if lost, issue in decadence. This is ours! And the weight of historical evidence is against our waking up. Whole civilizations will die, have died, rather than wake up! Must God raise up his seed of Abraham from another race? Must he whet his sword?

It would seem so, for now we are *numerous* enough to be a majority, *established* long enough to be comparatively unchallenged, *settled* enough that not even an earthquake disturbs our worship, *old* enough to have dignity, poise, and some beauty, *rich* enough to be social leaders, *powerful* enough to rewrite laws if we are hemmed too tightly, *content* enough to be beyond the reach of new social pressures, *pious* enough to know no real conviction for sin, *strong* enough to need no brothers, and *complacent* enough to be highly discriminating about the responsibilities we admit beyond ourselves. Hence, John's "bring forth therefore fruits worthy of your repentance" has its hard way to make among us. We do not look for new seed of Abraham—God has got us! Let him be content.

I. THE WORTH OF THE INDIVIDUAL

We were not always rich, or numerous, or powerful, or so sure of our chosen-ness.

Once there were fewer than thirty of us at Culpeper, Virginia, and our women wept at the blood dripping from our pastor's hands as he preached through the bars of the town gaol. Before that, once there were but four of us screaming to our executioners that we were not a part of that Muenster madness, but our bones bleached in a cage on the town hall roof for decades just the same. And once there was but one of us to whom our precious immersion-baptism was not only a "threat of death" but became death itself as Dame Hubmaier, strapped to her ducking stool, was buried "with Him" till she died. Not even in death could she have her companion, for Dr. Hubmaier got his from sulphur and fire. We have not all been so gently and genteelly baptized! And once, when there were more of us, we loaded our pathetic possessions on our ox-wagons and came to the high wilds of West Virginia and east Kentucky to escape the taxes and the sacraments of the state-supported Anglicans. For we have often bought our privacy and freedom at the price of isolation and ignorance.

But one of us took his ideas to James Madison and they got in the "Bill of Rights" for Virginia—and later they became the bedrock of our American system of personal freedom. Some of us got to school, even started schools, while others rode the back roads in early days. And in the forests, where a bear killed the first pastor of the first full-time church I served, today there is a little city full of adherents to his faith and ours. We won our way. God raised us up from stones—the stones of Maine whence Kittery's little congregation moved to Charleston, and the stones of Wales and England and from Holland's sand flats. We won our way to this that we have. On the backs of grand men preaching five grand ideas, we came to this.

The individual soul, in so far as any human agency is concerned, is both competent and responsible for his encounter with God in Christ. The church is composed of men who have so encountered God and who, by immersion in "believer's baptism," bear witness to such a meeting of grace. Such a company of believers is responsible to no earthly or churchly authority except Jesus Christ and its understanding of his will; while within that church all members are equal—no expertness bringing obeisance. Such a fellowship remains completely separate from the state, its cogs never meshing with the cogs of state, while its members live as citizens of two kingdoms. And finally, only the Scriptures provide for such a fellowship its authority in all matters of faith and practice.

Fundamental to each principle, underlying every one, is the great broad concept of the worth of any individual man, every individual man. Since every major tenet we held put us fairly in the center of the almost irresistible rise of the common man in this hemisphere, the "century of the common man" saw us lifted to an unbelievable level of size, power, wealth, and influence. But we left someone behind, and here appears the fundamental cleavage in our personality. Here appears the cleft that threatens to make us schizophrenic and calls for God to raise up from saner stones a people he can trust. We left someone behind, and in order to reconcile us, we added five principles to these others.

II. EROSION OF THE FUNDAMENTAL CONCEPT

Accursed day that ever we theologized and falsely biologized our great discrepancy!

About one hundred and twenty years ago when first we Baptists began to assume some place of numerical strength in the South, a fundamental contradiction between our mighty tenet—"all men have equal rights"—and our common practice—"some white men have equal rights"—began to appear to our conscience. The thing just didn't look right! Even though we brought hundreds of slaves into our communities and churches and called them "our people," it still did not look right. Yet, slavery for the "New South" was so vital an economic institution, and prosperity was so obviously God's desire for us, that it had to be right. There had to be an explanation, and there was.

In the mid-1800's we could not call biology to our rescue, for she was barely a science. In the South theology was queen of sciences, for astronomy and geology could not replace her without biology's help, and Darwin had not yet written. So, without Darwin to call on, we went a notch higher and used God. Theology would explain this contradiction—and it did, until biology came to bolster the spots where theology sagged at the seams.

God did this thing! He made races; he intended races; and we violate his will if we try to unmake anything he has made. He makes some superior and some inferior. Some are sons of Ham, "drawers of water," "hewers of wood." Let us not tamper with God's decree. And though such reasoning seeped through the seams of our consciences here and there, the theology did it, and survives a hundred years later to form the bulwark of the Dutch Reformed gasps at preserving economic superiority by means of "apartheid" in South Africa. They are preaching our 1840 theology!

Meanwhile Darwin came through, and modern biology was no longer the work of naturalists and bird-watchers. It became a *science*. And under the twisting of Huxley and Spencer, Darwin—poor Darwin—was made to claim claims he never dreamed. Malthus and Mendel and Darwin, what crimes were committed in their names! A word that once referred to families of flowers now began to be used in a new sense. *Race* came to mean a difference in color pigmentation of human hide, and there were other differences. Gobineau expanded them, Chamberlain copied Gobineau, Nietzsche used them to build Superman, and Hitler lived them into *Mein Kampf*. But worst of all, here in the South we Christians used a butchered biology to bolster a biased theology, and it threatens to destroy not only our major principle of equality, but our very personality as a people of God.

Since about 1875 a blend of poor theology and poorer biology has crystallized in our minds to form the five great principles of pseudo racism by which we preserve our vaunted superiority. They are every one as false as they are deadly. They all appear in the first volume of Gobineau's *Essay on the Differences in Races*. (Volumes II and III are still in French since we needed only Volume I.) And every single one has been offered by some "educator" during the past year as being the fruit of vast research and earnest inquiry. And worse, it is done and accepted with a straight face. But what are these vaunted principles by which racism thrives?

1. All cultural advance and, at bottom, all human prog-

ress are the work of and a result of the gifts of the great Aryan, primarily Germanic, predominantly Anglo-Saxon, race.

2. All other races, especially colored of any kind, derive their advantages from the Aryan race and by nature are imitators, except where they are despoilers.

3. Race itself means the existence of certain psychic differences as pronounced as physical differences and by these native traits, some races are "hewers of wood and drawers of water," incapable of better things.

4. Human prosperity requires within a culture the presence of a race of conquerors and a race of vanquished so that all types of functions may be filled. Aryan superiority being obvious, the racial disposition of the problem is the most obvious and the most profitable to the "superior" group.

5. Any race mixture is a mongrelization which breeds out the better race qualities of each group and leaves always an inferior product.

And so it goes. Last week a woman telephoned to ask if it were not true that any child of Negro-white parentage would have skin like a garfish; and a man asked earnestly if King David were not really Anglo-Saxon. Recently in Poland an old lady was quite upset to discover that Jesus had been a Jew—she had thought he was a Pole!

Meanwhile, modern anthropology knows nothing of any psychic characteristics of race. Modern sociology knows no intracultural tie-up of prejudice, for prejudice is everywhere a product of provincialism multiplied by institutionalism. There is no organic connection between race prejudice in South Africa and South Alabama. Modern biology knows no valid racism; there is only invalid stereotyping which refuses to see men as individuals and prefers to keep them in nice, safe categories. And most important, an honest biblical theology knows that *race* is strictly a modern concept, biologically and theologically false, for "God has made from one every nation. . . ."

Meanwhile, the cleavage is sharp in our consciences. We cannot ignore the economic, selfish fear that provokes our poor theology of racism. We cannot close off the emotional set of automatic switches that guarantees our automatic racial reactions. Nor can we forget that haunting, throbbing undertone caused by the deep vibrations of the great hope that led us to freedom—all men are born with equal rights. We begin to suspect that the Creator wills it so, and that the two-thirds of the earth's millions who are "colored" in our eyes will not continue too long to co-operate with our superiority. The tensions of Asia and Africa spill over into our county seat towns, our school boards, our deacons' meetings, our coffee houses. And it doesn't help at all that John the Baptist keeps telling us to "bring forth fruits worthy of our repentance."

III. AXE AT THE ROOT

Nor does it help for us to remind ourselves that we are strong enough, in God's grace, to fix it. And it frightens us that he may expect us to achieve this thing as the seed of Abraham. And sometimes we wake up in the night remembering that Ephesus, too, was a strong and mighty church when the angel of the Lord called her to "repent, else I come swiftly unto thee." Now, for nearly 1700 years, since the Goths came, Ephesus has been a heap, thirty miles from any house.

Meanwhile, twenty-seven rifle balls blaze through an old Negro woman's house as she prays in Gregg County. A month ago a Negro lad, with his new school clothes laid out to wear, and thirty dollars worth of cotton-picking money in his pockets, died from a .22 bullet fired at random from a car at the roadside stand where he stopped for his "soda-water." A pastor is "frozen out" for refusing to vote against his conscience; a thousand towns, in a thousand ways, continue the thousands of hurts to the spirit of man, and the hackles rise on trustees' necks if we ever get too "Christian."

We were not always rich. Once we were poor, but how strange the ways of a minority people when they have grown to a majority! Sometimes we forget the principle whose throbbings gave us birth. When we do, John says, we lose our heritage. Does the axe now lie at the root of the tree? This thing that lies before us is no "illustration" of the gospel's claim. It is its prime expression in our time and a new kind of Pentecost lies beyond it.

Meanwhile, is there hope? Thin and well-grayed at fifty-five, two children in the university, all money gone, modest salary, small town church, eyes puffed with worry and fatigue, and in tears, he said, "I'll vote my conscience if it kills me." In him and his kind who keep speaking their piece, there is hope, high hope, all we have. We get our peace when we achieve it, not before.

Once we were weak and had a great high love: the belief that in our Lord Christ's name men are really men, ends in themselves, never means to an end. And once the great church at Ephesus heard: "Nevertheless I have somewhat against thee, because thou hast left thy first love. Remember therefore from whence thou art fallen, and repent, and do the first works, or else I will come unto thee."

Maranatha!

Even so, come Lord Jesus, and show us how to do this great thing.

What Would Jesus Have Us Do?

PHILIPPIANS 1:27; 2:5

R. LOFTON HUDSON

The religion of Jesus Christ is being challenged in our day as it has been few times in history. About one-third of our world professes to be atheistic. Standards of morality (particularly in sex) are changing so rapidly that even counselors are confused. Nations clasp right hands in mock friendship and with their left hands rearrange cobalt bombs. Whole national groups close their doors to Christian missionaries. In this context our interpretation of what it means to follow Christ today must be re-examined.

What *does* it mean? Does being a Christian make any difference in the way we act when social issues arise? Do Christians have a better sense of justice and fair play than non-Christians? Do we love our neighbors better than pagans love them? From reading the New Testament, one would expect the followers of Jesus to be the most unselfish, the most reasonable, the most concerned, the most loving people on earth. But are they?

Our text in the words of J. B. Phillips is timeless counsel from Paul: "Whatever happens, make sure that your everyday life is worthy of the Gospel of Christ. . . . Let Christ Himself be your example as to what your attitude should be." The words "everyday life" and "your attitude" stand out in my mind. It is following Christ every day that

85

credits or discounts our religion. Since our attitudes determine our conduct, Christ wants to change us at the very center of our being. Under his tutelage and with his power we will translate his message into day-by-day practice.

If we believe that Christ is profoundly interested in everything that affects man—the least, the lost, and the last —we must ask ourselves about all issues, "What would Jesus have us do?"

Let us follow this question as we confront one of the most controversial issues of our day: racial segregation in the public schools.

I. JESUS IS INTERESTED IN THIS PROBLEM

First, Christians cannot talk about this problem without getting involved in interpreting the Golden Rule, the parable of the good Samaritan, the second great commandment, "love thy neighbour as thyself," and the like. The way we think of our fellow man, and the way we treat him, is a basic concern of the Sermon on the Mount. Jesus is interested in this problem because of his love for *all* men.

Second, Jesus is aware of the difficulties involved. He sees that politicians are trying to "make hay" out of this issue. He knows how deep our prejudices are, and how long-standing. He sees the difficulties in Southern communities where the Negro population is from 30 to 70 per cent. He knows that economic disadvantages have handicapped the Negro educationally and hygienically. He loves white men, too, and yearns for them to respect their colored brothers.

Third, I think Jesus is interested in the principles that are being applied in our schools because in this competing world of ours, the Christian faith is being measured beside both communistic atheism and the ethnic religions. The constitution of the Republic of India, thanks largely to Mahatma Gandhi, has ruled out the caste system. After centuries of stigma for millions, "untouchability" seems to be on its way out. Of course communism has won many adherents by insisting that there are no class or race distinctions in their scheme of things.

In 1950 UNESCO published a book entitled *What Is Race? Evidence from Scientists.* This great international organization came to the conclusion that races are so mixed that the term "race" had better be dropped from usage, that there are no cultural traits that are connected with a particular race as such. This is basically what every reputable scientist has been saying for fifty years. But the apostle Paul said this about nineteen hundred years ago, on Mars' Hill in Athens. There really is but one race, the human race.

Now, my point is this. Can we allow the Hindus, the Communists, or the United Nations to hold a more defensible position on this point than the churches of Jesus Christ do? Acknowledging Jesus as the Son of God, we cannot admit to a higher standard than his.

This leads to a fourth reason for saying that Christ is interested in this problem. Ask any Christian missionary to any land on earth how other peoples feel about our segregation of Negroes.

The late Dr. M. Theron Rankin, one-time missionary to China and executive secretary of Southern Baptist foreign mission work, once declared: "More and more the sincerity of our interest in the colored peoples within their native lands will be judged by our treatment of the peoples of those lands who live in our country." Undoubtedly the Christian missionary witness in Africa is greatly hindered by our treatment of the Negroes in our beloved Southland.

Segregation is for the Christian not simply a political or civil matter. It is a religious issue. At least I am my brother's brother (even my colored brother), and at times I am his keeper.

II. THE SIZE OF THE PROBLEM

Now let us look back for a moment at the historical background of our problem. In 1619 the first Negro slaves landed in Virginia. In 1847 Sarah Roberts, a Negro girl in Boston, brought suit because she was barred from the nearest public school. The Supreme Court held that the practice of separate schools for Negroes did not in itself constitute discrimination. Then followed the bloody Civil War and the terrible days of Reconstruction in the South. For years public education was greatly handicapped.

Since most schools in the South were for white children, Northern philanthropy came to the aid of the Negro schools. Between 1913 and 1932, for example, the Julius Rosenwald Fund helped finance the building of 5,000 Negro schools in fifteen Southern and border states. Negro education gradually came to have better facilities and better teachers, especially from 1930. Harry S. Ashmore has presented a factual study of school conditions for Negroes in his *The Negro and the Schools* published in 1955 by the University of North Carolina Press.

As a human being and as a citizen in a democracy, however, the Negro could not be satisfied with "separate but equal" status. It labeled him as not worthy to attend the same schools as the rest of us. In spite of all our reasoning about why Negroes and whites could not go to the same school, the principle and practice of segregation was unacceptable.

On May 17, 1954, the Supreme Court delivered one of

the most courageous decisions in its history. Separate schools for Negro children must go. But even this was not entirely new. Before this date eighty-four Southern institutions of higher education had already acted to eliminate the racial bar to enrolment, and among them were a number of denominational colleges and seminaries. Segregation in schools had been troubling our consciences for some time.

To date, however, the problem is far from solved. Six states continue their segregation policies. Probably before another year is passed, some of these six will relent. Those of us who live in desegregated states should remember one thing: we are not more righteous than our deep-South brothers. It little becomes us to thank God that we are not as prejudiced as others, for some still nurse resentment against Jews, Mexicans, and Orientals.

Solving the segregation problem will not be easy in some places, especially where the non-white population is above 10 per cent, and where the economic level of the Negro is very low. We should remember, too, that this Supreme Court decision will not solve our racial tensions. We do not suddenly overcome decades of prejudice and conflict. Of an especially vicious kind of evil spirit dwelling in the life of a certain man's lunatic son, Jesus once said, "This kind goeth not out but by prayer and fasting" (Matt. 17:21).

III. WHAT WOULD JESUS HAVE US DO?

The Negro-white situation in the United States threatens our moral and political leadership in the world. Two-thirds of the people of the earth are colored. Many of these listen to us talk of democracy and sneer at us as despicable hypocrites. It is bad enough to fail to practice what we preach, but to go back on our Christian idealism, to try to use the Bible to justify our prejudices, this is downright apostasy. The time has come for us Christians to say whether our Lord has anything to say on such knotty problems as the treatment of the colored one-tenth of our population.

Jesus stated his principles clearly, and his will is eternal in its application. None of us will practice it perfectly, but God forbid that we should pervert it. What would he have us do about this problem?

1. *We should not call any man common or unclean.* You remember the revelation to Simon Peter at Joppa? Read again the story in Acts 10. Its point is that Peter and other Jewish Christians looked upon Gentiles as inferior human beings, but Peter learned that "God is no respecter of persons."

This is the message of the remainder of the New Testament and, for that matter, of the Old Testament as well. James went so far as to say that "if ye have respect to persons, ye commit sin" and violate what he calls the royal law. "Thou shalt love thy neighbour as thyself" (James 2:1–9).

Here we are at the heart of our school integration problem. The famous Southern sociologist, the late Dr. Howard Odum, has pointed out that "it is of the utmost importance that Southerners face the plain assumption that they do not appraise the Negro as the same sort of human beings as they themselves are." [1] Can this be true in our Bible-reading South?

Some will say that the Negro cannot learn as fast, that he shows up poorly on intelligence tests, that his moral

---

[1] Howard Odum, "An Approach to Diagnosis and Direction of the Problem of Negro Segregation in the Public Schools," *Journal of Public Law,* Vol. 3, No. 1, Spring, 1954.

standards are lower, and that he has other inherent weaknesses. Even if these were true, are we thereby relieved from obeying the Bible? In thinking of a group of people as "common or unclean," we violate God's law. Education cannot solve this problem. Only repentance can.

Jesus expressly forbade such labeling, as an act of hostility. Listen to him:

You have heard that it was said to the men of old, "You shall not kill; and whoever kills shall be liable to judgment." But I say to you that every one who is angry with his brother shall be liable to judgment; whoever insults his brother shall be liable to the council, and whoever says, "You fool!" shall be liable to the hell of fire. So if you are offering your gift at the altar, and there remember that your brother has something against you, leave your gift there before the altar and go; first be reconciled to your brother, and then come and offer your gift. Make friends quickly with your accuser, while you are going with him to court, lest your accuser hand you over to the judge, and the judge to the guard, and you be put in prison; truly, I say to you, you will never get out till you have paid the last penny.   MATTHEW 5:21–26 RSV

Two things are found in this passage. First, name-calling is condemned. Yet many Christian ministers and Sunday school teachers talk about "Niggers." Can it be that they do not know that self-respecting Negroes object to that name? Or do they not care?

When our churches and Christian homes stop telling jokes which hold Negroes up to ridicule, when we learn to use the courteous, respectful titles in addressing them—such as, Mr., Mrs., and Miss—we will be on the way toward working out our "school problem." Until we practice these courtesies, we ought to admit our sin. If I read Matthew 5 correctly, some professing Christians are in grave danger of hell fire. Jesus must have meant exactly what he said. If we do not have love in our hearts, we will end up in hell—all "piosity" and tithing notwithstanding. This does not mean that we have to be perfect in order to be saved. But it does mean that Christ must be in our hearts, and if he lives there, we will not be satisfied to attach labels to people—Nigger, fool, or anything to belittle them. Rejection of another as a person, hate in any form, is a movement toward murder, and is dangerous. That is what Jesus was saying.

The rest of this passage shows how to deal with just such a problem as integration. "If thou rememberest that thy brother has aught against thee"—we can never forget what the "aught" is so far as the Negro is concerned.

But we white Christians waited too long. The Supreme Court had to tell us. Christ forgive us for this neglect! Surely, the least we can do is to sit down with our Negro brothers and try now to be reconciled with them.

2. *We ought to live by the Golden Rule.* What does it mean? That we should put ourselves in the other person's place and say, "How would this look to me if I were a Negro and thinking straight?"

When a white man asked a Negro leader what he and his white friends could do for the Negro race, his answer was simple: "Just imagine that you and your family are Negroes." He did. First, he realized that he would have to move out of the neighborhood in which he was living. His son could not enter the medical school of his choice. He must answer a thousand "whys" that his children would ask him about their inferior privileges with, "We were born Negroes."

It takes only a little imagination for any of us to see what the Supreme Court meant when it said: "To separate them (Negroes) from others of similar age and qualifications solely because of their race generates a feeling of inferiority as to their status in the community that may affect their hearts and minds in a way not likely ever to be undone." This suggests what Jesus meant by "Do unto others." If *we* would not want to be Negroes, because of discriminatory practices, we must change these practices.

It must be admitted that in many sections of the South the Negro's standards of speech, cleanliness, dress, and work habits are very different from those of the white people. These conditions are nobody's fault in particular, they are usually the haphazard result of economic turmoil and deprivation.

The question is, what is the Christian approach to the limitations of the Negroes in a particular community? Do these Scripture passages apply? "Freely ye have received, freely give." "Bear ye one another's burdens, and so fulfil the law of Christ." "Look not every man on his own things, but every man also on the things of others." "I have shewed you all things, how that so labouring ye ought to support the weak, and to remember the words of the Lord Jesus, how he said, It is more blessed to give than to receive."

This problem of segregation in the schools should cause every born-again person to seek as never before to be thoroughly Christian. In our looks, our speech, our associations, our every relationship, we need to practice the Golden Rule. It will take real Christian grace to do it, but our God is able to help. This attempt at integration can well be the most stimulating factor, in terms of moral alertness, that has happened in this century.

3. *Having been saved by redeeming love, we are to practice Christian love.* Love was Jesus' message and his way of life. It still is. When he challenges us on this point,

will we go away from him as the crowds did? The crowds have always done one of two things regarding Jesus' teachings on love: water them down until they become practically meaningless or ignore the whole message as impractical.

Love is a personal experience of unselfish concern and respect for another. Does one accept the other person as valuable? Does he reverence him as a creature of God bearing his special image? Does he accept this person's uniqueness (color, form, habits, talents) as God endows him? Does he care about the other's welfare? Will he help him, yet leave him free to make his own mistakes and become his true self?

Dr. Paul Tillich of Harvard has pointed out that "love is the drive towards the unity of the separated. Reunion presupposes separation of that which belongs essentially together. . . . It is impossible to unite that which is *essentially* separated. Without an ultimate belongingness no union of one thing with another can be conceived." [2] God and man belong together. Man and man belong together, not staring across wide gulfs of misunderstanding and injustice, not peeping through iron or bamboo curtains at each other's store of munitions.

This "togetherness" does not mean that we must join hands with everyone in every phase of our lives. This is impossible. But it would seem to mean that we must be free, first of all, to form whatever relationships we wish. The man in the prison and jail has forfeited this right. He has proved himself incapable of playing the game by the rules.

The desegregation of the schools simply sets the stage

[2] *Love, Power and Justice* (New York: Oxford University Press, 1954) p. 25.

for enough freedom to be together. To restrict people who are like ourselves breeds hate. To bring them together will not produce Christian love, but it will bring about love only in Christians who are mature enough to see the opportunity to love.

In Christ's day there were three great lines of cleavage: race, social status, and sex. Racially there were Jews and Gentiles, Greeks and barbarians; Jesus crossed this boundary in Samaria and in his treatment of a centurion. In social status there were many divisions, slave and freedman, rich and poor, religious and sinners. Everyone knows how Jesus rose above these differences. As for sex distinctions, his natural, respectful treatment of women has inspired reforms through Christendom.

We know that in the Christian churches the problem of segregation did not arise until the seventeenth century. In the early days of the church, Christians were known as a "third race." All were included in its fellowship. Segregation is a modern problem, but it is not too modern for Christ. His principle of love applies with genuine meaning to this as well as all other human relations.

Jesus is calling us to lead the way in every program of justice and love. We must not live merely under law but under grace. If the Supreme Court can direct a change in our public schools, we ought to be the ones to show how Christian love can make it work. Our Master once asked, "What do ye more than others?" If you are kind to those of your own race only, how can you call yourselves Christians? Do not unbelievers do that well, and some of them better than we? "Be ye therefore perfect, even as your Father which is in heaven is perfect." He sends the sun and the rain on Negroes as well as on white men. Perhaps along the way, we may learn how to sit beside them in the classroom, play with them on the ball diamond; and some of us may thereby help the world to believe in the power of Christ to change our small hearts.

It was Nietzsche who said, "There has been only one Christian on the earth and he died on a cross." And George Bernard Shaw remarked that there is much to be said for Christianity, especially if the world, after two thousand years of violence, should give Christianity a trial. Such cynics are standing at every corner. They are watching us Christians to see if our "everyday life is worthy of the Gospel of Christ." Our God is saying to us, "Let Christ Himself be your example as to what your attitude should be."

Segregation is a religious problem for those of us who propose to be followers of the lowly Nazarene. All of us need to be humble and aggressive and intelligent in facing it. To read each other out of the synagogue over it is not Christian. To do nothing about it is impossible now. To fall on our faces before God and ask for his wisdom is imperative. In the meantime, let us do what Jesus would have us do in our community.

The Spiritual Significance of Work | 11

JOHN 5:17

CHARLES A. TRENTHAM

Strange and baffling, isn't it, that so much of God's power is channeled through men? At the pool of Bethesda lay an impotent man. So long had he lain there that despair close to utter imbecility was written all over his face. Near by was the healing pool of God. Only one thing was lacking—the work of one man to put him into the pool.

It is one of the great paradoxes of the Christian faith that we believe in a God who has all power but who says unashamedly, "I have need of thee." We believe in a God who existed from all eternity, who had no need of a birth to exist and yet borrowed a stable in which to be born; a God who haunted the conscience of man from the dawn of creation, who was the living Word whispering to every listening heart and yet a God who borrowed a boat from which to preach his gospel. We believe in a God who borrowed an upper room in which to talk about his Father's house of many mansions; a God who says, "All power hath been given unto me in heaven and in earth," and yet calls the church his body and confesses that he is paralyzed unless his members move. Perhaps the purpose behind this paradox is that man might have the high and holy privilege of working with God.

97

Our text is: "My Father worketh even until now, and I work" (John 5:17 ASV). It tells us three things about work: God the Father works; Christ the Son works; and the implication is that all who are made in their image and live in their fellowship must also work.

I. GOD THE FATHER WORKS

The great distinguishing characteristic which set Israel's God apart from the gods of all other nations is that Israel's God is not an aristocrat. He is a working God. Jesus said, "My Father worketh." He not only created the universe, but he is the sustainer of all natural processes and all living things. "In him we live, and move, and have our being." In the story before us God had worked in healing a cripple. The healing of the physical side of life was thus regarded by our Lord as the work of God. We may, therefore, conclude that the work of God is not purely spiritual. It also includes action in the physical realm.

In fact, the common dualism which separates the physical from the spiritual in an absolute way, which has come to be so much a part of our thinking, was never in the mind of Jesus. All life was sacred to him. He drew no line between the sacred and the secular. To him even the body was the temple of the Holy Spirit. It was only after Christianity had invaded the Western world and passed through the processes of dualistic Greek philosophy that Christians began to think of the physical side of life as being evil. The Hebrew believed that even his body would be raised to share in eternal life. The material things of life were sacred in the eyes of Jesus. He regarded them as gifts from God. Rather than declaring them to be unimportant or evil, he actually said, "Your heavenly Father knoweth that ye have need of all these things."

Furthermore, our Lord did not divide work into two categories and call the one sacred and the other secular. Some tasks he regarded as having priority over others. He said, "Seek ye first the kingdom of God"; however, he regarded all honest work as sacred.

Furthermore, next to the evil of shutting God out of our world is the evil of shutting him out of our work by regarding what we do in the church as God's work and what we do outside the church as our own affair. This philosophy has found so wide a range among young people that many have felt that the only lives dedicated to God are those in the pastoral ministry or in the missionary service of the church.

Jesus said, "Lift up your eyes, and look on the fields; for they are white already unto harvest." This passage has so often been used as the basis for an appeal for missionaries to carry the gospel to foreign lands that its original meaning has been lost. Our Lord was thinking of a spiritual harvest in that wicked city immediately before them. He was thinking of the harvest that had just been gathered in the conversion of a wicked woman who in turn evangelized the city by sharing the good news of one who knew all about her past but also knew glorious things about her future. The white harvest was not to be gathered by professional religionists. The land of Palestine was already over-burdened by the numerous priests who gained their livelihood through ministering one week out of the year in the Temple. The great need was for dedicated men and women into whose hearts the transforming grace of God had so come that they were moved to share spontaneously the wondrous good tidings of God's love.

Another attendant evil of the philosophy which divides the sacred from the secular is that many have been led to believe that by doing a certain amount of "sacred" work around the church they may be excused for their ruthless practices in business or for their questionable social lives. Perhaps this accounts for the fact that the church has failed to carry the gospel into the economic realm. We have said that religion exists for the purpose of building the organizations of the church and that the only sacred work is that which is directly concerned with building the organizational life of the church. Over against this stands the New Testament declaring that God is supremely interested in redeeming the world. The church that barricades herself behind her own walls and moves in egocentric organizational circles ceases to be the church of the Redeemer.

Not until we come to see that all honest work has the halo of heaven around it will the leaven of the gospel permeate our whole economic structure as Christ intended. Religion, if it is adequate, must concern itself with the routine labors of life and not simply with the high hours of holy elation. Pity the man whose soul never soars to the heights in worship, but pity also the man who has never discovered that source of strength which sustains him through the toil of his common task.

Our text tells us that God works like a father. "My Father worketh. . . ." A father delights to work for his family. Have you ever thought of how extravagant God was when he created our world? The grass of the field was a necessity to sustain the animal life that feeds upon it, but the wild flowers are a part of the superfluous bounty of God. The flowers made to blush unseen and shed their fragrance on the desert air show that God is not a utilitarian. He created beauty for the joy of it and because works of beauty are a part of that kingdom not made with hands. The sun that bathes the earth with golden glory is necessary to life, but the moon that sails in majesty and beauty through the night to lend the light of enchantment and romance to the resting world is a part of God's gracious extravagance. Archibald Rutledge has said, "The wind is perhaps a necessity, but the song that it croons through the morning pines is a different thing." The lavish beauty of this earth reveals the joy which God experienced from his handiwork.

Dr. Charles Mayo had a motto which he hung on the wall of his office. Here it is: "There is no fun like work." He wrote, "I have always liked that motto for I believe in it. To be without work is almost to be without life. For it is work which creates interest in life."

II. CHRIST THE SON WORKS

The second great affirmation of our text is that Christ the Son works. "My Father worketh even until now, and I work." Since God the Father is not an aristocrat, Christ is not the son of an aristocrat. He joins his Father in the great fellowship of labor. He came as a servant with a basin and a towel saying, "Whosoever will be chief among you, let him be your servant." He said the only ambition worth having is the ambition to work for the good of others.

He acknowledged no small jobs and no little people. The introduction of a current book says, "Concerning the phrase, 'the little people,' I regard this phrase as patronizing and repulsive. There are no little people in this book. They are as big as you are, whoever you are." All men in the eyes of Jesus were potential sons of the King of heaven.

Standing before the great cathedral of Cologne, a tourist heard a voice saying, "Didn't we do a fine piece of work here?" She turned to see a plain working man. "What did you do about it," she asked. "I mixed the mortar across the street for two years," was his cheerful reply. What sort of building would that great cathedral be were it not for mortar-mixers? Then thank God if your life is cast among the mortar-mixers. Christ in a carpenter's shop lived in that lowly fellowship of men who toiled with their hands. If you would live in his fellowship today you will find him in the servant's quarters of his own universe.

Our Lord was able to work leisurely. His life was not hurried or hectic. The girl who made it through a great art gallery in thirty minutes and would have made it in twenty except for her high heels is a symbol of our age. Over against that stands the marvelous serenity of Jesus. You cannot read the opening chapters of Mark's Gospel without being positively amazed at how much Jesus was able to do in one day; yet you never get the impression that he was ever very busy. He simply did that which was at hand as though it would be the last thing he ever did; then he went on to his next responsibility in the full assurance that the God who had appointed his task would provide the strength for its fulfilment. He never doubted that God's grace would provide everything that God demanded of his children.

Furthermore, our Lord worked with joyous spontaneity. He never begrudged the necessity of hard toil. He knew that work itself was to be enjoyed and not simply regarded as a means to an end. Many of us never throw ourselves into our work with high enthusiasm and deep devotion because we think of it as an evil ordeal to be endured for the sake of that which it produces. It becomes a means of earning a living rather than a real part of that life which is in fellowship with the divine Toiler.

To work under the grip of a great inspiration is one of

the sublime joys of life. Last summer I sat in the great Westminster Central Hall in London and thought of those perilous days when Winston Churchill called the miners of Britain to assemble there. A great crisis had arisen. It was just after Dunkirk and the miners were not getting out the coal. From all over the Island they came pouring into London by plane, bus, and train. By Saturday morning three thousand miners filled the Hall.

The Prime Minister arose and said, "I want to give it to you straight. You know after Dunkirk we had nothing. I give it to you straight—nothing—two hundred guns, no more; twenty tanks, that's all. I heard he was coming with a million men, [he referred to Hitler as "he"] and I said to myself, 'The British Navy will put five hundred thousand of them to the bottom of the Channel, but what will we do with half a million of them ashore?' " For an hour and forty minutes he outlined the desperate situation confronting Britain. Then in stirring language unsurpassed in the annals of oratory, he said, "When at last it's over, we'll parade these streets again and as you go by people will call out, 'and where were you?' Someone will answer, 'I marched with the Eighth Army,' and someone else will say, 'I was in the skies over Britain.' Another will reply, 'I was in the Merchant Marine pushing the ships through the sea up to Archangel.' Then I shall be standing there and I shall see you marching by, the coal miners of Britain, and I will call out, 'where were you?' I will hear you answer, 'We were down in the black of the pits right up against the face of the coal.' "

"Then," said Dr. Sangster, who related the story, "with a voice full of emotion, three thousand British coal miners arose and with tears streaming down their faces cheered the Prime Minister, and the coal came out."

Men who work with the grip and inspiration of a great purpose know a joy that is indescribable.

III. THE CHRISTIAN WORKS WITH GOD

The major implication of the text is that since God is a worker, all who live in the fellowship of God must work. The central doctrine of the New Testament is that Christ moves into every trusting heart to take control and to restore the image of God in the soul. To be made like God makes man a fellow laborer with God.

Perhaps the reason many of our American products are so poorly made is that we do not realize that we are fellow laborers with God and should, therefore, feel the responsibility for producing that which would honor the God who works through us by providing skill and energy for all our labors.

The story is told of an Italian duke who was strolling through his garden in the early morning. He came upon a workman toiling among the flowers. Startled to have his solitude broken he asked, "What are you doing here at this hour of the morning?"

"I'm making a box for the flowers," was the reply.

"But why are the carvings so intricate and the fittings so perfect? The use of the box does not demand such perfection."

"But," said the workman, "my spirit does."

"Then," said the Duke, "you are wasting your time on such meaningless toil."

"The Carpenter of Nazareth would never have made anything less than perfect."

The Duke was offended. "You shall be flogged for your impudence! What is your name?"

"I am Michelangelo, sir."

The motive behind all worthy toil should be to fulfil the will of him who never makes anything less than perfect. Even these personalities of ours will one day be made after his own image. A little child who had been born physically deformed came to the age when she was sensitive about it. She looked forlornly up into her mother's face and asked, "Mother, why did God make me like this?" With deep spiritual discernment the mother replied, "My child, God isn't through making you."

Paul tells us that God has begun a good work in us and will surely bring it to completion. If we are being made in his image, then our work must reflect some of the beauty and perfection of God.

We who believe so profoundly in salvation by grace have often been afraid of a gospel of work. We have feared that man might forget that there is nothing that he can do to merit God's favor. That is a wholesome fear. But the grace of God is not simply the unmerited favor of God. It is also that power that moves into the human soul to make us gracious even as God is gracious and to dispose us to work for the good of others when they could no more merit it than we could merit the grace of God.

The true evidence that we are children of grace is that we are gracious towards others. While it is true that we are not saved by working, it is also true that we are not saved if we do not work. Does not James teach us that the faith that saves is the faith that works? "Show me thy faith without thy works, and I will show thee my faith by my works." The highest faith was expressed by those shining words of Jesus, "My Father worketh even until now and I work."

LUKE 15:11–32

NOLAN P. HOWINGTON

Jesus dramatized the problem of juvenile delinquency in the story of the prodigal son. With real discernment he described a youth who revolted against the authority and discipline of the home, who squandered his money and his energies in a quest for social status and personal satisfaction. Reduced to poverty and hunger, he retraced his steps to his childhood home to receive forgiveness and restoration at the hands of his father.

Many of our modern youth have a kinship with that prodigal boy. Juvenile delinquents have become headline news across the nation. The morning paper may tell of a fourteen-year-old lad who, under the influence of narcotics, murdered his grandmother,[1] or it may describe the vandalism, sadism, and recklessness of youth groups. The behavior problem among our youthful citizens is a serious one, and it merits the attention of legal, educational, social, and religious leaders.

The multiplicity of opinions about teen-age crime reflects the confusion of observers concerning its causes and cures. In many respects social workers, police officers and judges, columnists and religious leaders have resembled the blind men who surrounded the elephant, each one identifying the animal in terms of the bodily part that he

[1] *Arkansas Gazette*, Little Rock, Arkansas, November 1, 1955.

happened to touch! The elephant, however, is more than a leg, a trunk, or a tail. Juvenile delinquency is a complex social problem that will not yield to superficial analysis or simple single-track solutions. It arises from an endless number of causes and is amenable to several preventive measures.

I. THE EXTENT OF JUVENILE DELINQUENCY

How much teen-age crime is there in our American culture? In the United States, since 1950, population has increased 5 per cent; crime has increased 20 per cent. In 1953 the adult crime rate increased 1.9 per cent while the crime rate of children under eighteen increased 7.9 per cent. According to F. B. I. statistics half of those arrested for burglary in 1953 were under eighteen years of age; 17 per cent of the nation's known drug addicts were under twenty-one; 15 per cent of the country's murderers were not yet twenty-one years old![2] "Only two per cent of the country's juvenile age group become delinquent each year," commented a social scientist, "and that is a small price to pay for our dynamic culture." But the "small price" represents one million youngsters between the ages of ten and seventeen who are handled by police officers. About 450,000 of these have been reaching the juvenile courts, contributing to a 45 per cent increase in the rate of juvenile delinquency in the past five years. This is five times the increase in population for this age group![3]

These young offenders are tomorrow's criminals, for the adult criminal world draws its recruits from the ranks of miscreant youth. Such a large segment of young life can-

[2] "Juvenile Delinquency" (editorial), *Christian Century* (Sept. 14, 1955), pp. 1045–57.
[3] R. V. McCann, "The Parable of the Delinquent Son," *Christian Century* (Oct. 5, 1955), p. 1139.

not with the approval of serious citizens be turned over to criminal careers. Each juvenile offender is a precious human being created for a life of usefulness and for fellowship with God. He is a jewel set, not for the swine's snout or the rubbish heap, but to glisten in beauty and righteousness before the Heavenly Father. The churches as well as the families and the law courts of the land have a stake in the conservation of youth. No earnest Christian will be content with pious platitudes and worn clichés. We need only to examine some of the causes of juvenile delinquency to realize the magnitude of this social problem and the difficulty of meeting its challenge.

II. CAUSES OF JUVENILE DELINQUENCY

What are the factors that contribute to delinquency among teen-agers? Albert Deutsch says that "delinquency has been attributed to every thing from solar disturbances to original sin." [4] Recently a New York judge, in a study of youthful offenders, listed thirteen specific causes of their crimes. Nearly all of these causative factors were related to failures within the family.[5] Widespread family disturbance is conducive to youth crimes. The Gluecks, outstanding team of sociologists, after analyzing 1,000 actual cases of juvenile delinquency, arrived at a similar conclusion. The story of many delinquents is one of family strife, divorce, desertion, parental indifference and rejection, crowded conditions, parental excesses in the use of alcohol, and an absence of ethical idealism.[6] Congested quar-

[4] Albert Deutsch, *Our Rejected Children* (Boston: Little, Brown & Co., 1950), p. 175.

[5] Walter D. Cavert, "News of the Christian World," *Christian Century* (Sept. 28, 1955), p. 1122.

[6] See Richard Clendenen, "When Teen-Agers Go Wrong," *U. S. News and World Report* (Sept. 17, 1954), p. 82; Paul H. Landis, *Adolescence and Youth* (New York: McGraw-Hill, 1945), p. 216.

ters in deteriorated neighborhoods provide a fertile soil for delinquency.

But the loveless and pagan homes in the exclusive suburbs, devoid of sane discipline, affection, and moral training, also spawn young lawbreakers. Millions of American children and youth are the victims of spiritual starvation and religious illiteracy. Frequently parents may be emotionally and morally unfit because of their own early training in disturbed family groups. They were poor marriage risks from the beginning, apt to perpetuate the sorry patterns of family life that they themselves had experienced.

Within every home there must be a recognition of the authority vested in parents. Wise parents will not relinquish control of their children. It is the role of the father and mother to guide the growth of the child lovingly but firmly. Discipline is an unpopular word in our restless and unrestrained society, and many homes accord children and youth a free hand in their choices, conduct, and selection of values. A youngster's welfare is never secured by removing the bridle and turning him loose in the open field! The weak, ignorant, or inadequate parent may not have patience and skill enough to impose wise restraints and give loving guidance to the child. Juvenile delinquency is related to the decrease in home discipline, the lack of cohesiveness within the family, and the removal of both parents from the home during a greater part of the child's waking hours. It is generally agreed that the industrial employment of women, taking the mother away from the children, has been a most disrupting influence within the home.

Children get their first impressions of law and order, honesty and decency within the family circle. They are influenced by the attitudes of parents either in the direction of truthfulness and honesty or deceitfulness and dishonesty. The spread of juvenile delinquency is related to the violation of the legal and moral code by adults. Youngsters assume that their misdeeds are no worse than the cocktail hour in their home, the traffic violations and tax evasions of which their fathers boast, and the quick money that came through a sharp business deal. Many parents have failed to inculcate into their children a respect for honesty, sobriety, and law.

Another source of juvenile misbehavior is the cultural environment into which our children are born and reared. Ours is a dynamic society characterized by mobility, change, restlessness, and the breakdown of familiar restraints. The twentieth century has witnessed the rapid growth of cities, the urbanization of life, the diminishing of personal relationships, and the congestion of many family groups in blighted urban areas.

In many sectors, the materialistic aims of our sensate culture have supplanted the Christian ideals or have sought the sanction and blessing of the church. Expediency and force, craftiness and greed too often replace honesty and diligence, kindness and generosity. The casual view that many youngsters assume toward wrongdoing is deeply disturbing to the Christian conscience. A young soldier came into my office at the regimental chapel in Camp Shelby, Mississippi. He was in trouble. His girl friend was pregnant, and he was torn between a sense of guilt and a desire to run out on her. The fact that he was troubled at all was a tribute to his previous Christian training. But the further fact that he finally dismissed the whole affair with a flippant remark, "I guess it's just one of those things," reflects the lackadaisical view of multitudes toward the violation of the Christian code of ethics. In many ways ours is a godless culture in which the bells toll out the death of decency, sobriety, and moral idealism.

This unsettled age, shaken to the core by global wars, revolutions, economic depression, military conscription, and changes in the sex code, has left its mark on all our people. Youth has suffered from being caught up in the uncertainty, tension, and conflict over ideals. The modern mind has revolted against constituted authority, and youth has shared the revolt. Whether the authority of a parent, a policeman, a legal statute, or a moral code, restraint has been unpopular and unwelcome.

William Healy has described the United States as "the most crime-ridden civilization in the world." [7] The Federal Bureau of Investigation in 1948 estimated that on the average a serious crime occurred somewhere in the land every 18.7 seconds, and in 1954 it estimated that there were 2,267,250 major crimes committed, or one every 13.9 seconds. Many of these crimes were committed by persons whose careers as lawbreakers dated back to childhood. "One half of our adult criminals begin their careers as juvenile delinquents." [8] A culture that produces an army of youthful violators each year needs the corrective of the Christian gospel!

Crime is a popular theme in the production of our media of mass communication and entertainment. It is popularized and glamorized through television, radio, movies, and comic books. Our children drink from the poisoned waters of this cultural well and grow up in a society whose main emphasis seems to be on getting someplace with little concern about the means used in getting there. It is the task of homes, schools, and churches to change the character

[7] Quoted by Deutsch, *op. cit.*, p. 279.
[8] Clendenen, *op. cit.*, p. 82.

of this society, to insure the proper moral and spiritual development of our children. Why are some children within a given area or family delinquent while others are not? Are there causative factors at the personal level that account for teen-age crime? It is never easy to understand the dynamics of human nature. But emotional disturbances, so severe as to demand psychiatric care, sometimes lie back of youthful misdeeds. The individual's desire for attention and status may be satisfied by delinquent acts. Such conduct may express the youngster's resentment over being rejected, his desire to strike out at the adult world, or his attempt to gain a place for himself with the gang.

Another factor, often overlooked because it is theological, is human propensity toward sin. Each person born into the world has within him a bias toward sin. This element in human nature is fostered and nurtured by the forces of organized evil which are intrenched in our social order. A neuro-psychiatrist once remarked that many of his patients were troubled by "asinic, assertive, aggressive neurosis." When asked for a simpler statement, he declared, "They are full of the devil!" That is often the explanation for the conduct of both adults and juveniles!

III. WE CAN SAVE OUR YOUTH

The cures and preventive measures suggested for juvenile delinquency are about as numerous as the causes that are sometimes listed. It must be remembered that we cannot deal with boys and girls as we would with stray dogs and cats! They cannot simply be taken from the streets and retained in institutions or put in isolation. Many of them do need psychiatric and institutional care. The corrective institution, however, may rehabilitate and save the youth, but statistics indicate that it is more likely to confirm him in a criminal career. We need to restudy our methods of handling youthful offenders. The churches are interested not in penalizing but in saving people. Christian zeal must be combined with scientific technique in the treatment of those who have violated the social and moral code. Mere verbalization—deploring the situation and repeating pious platitudes—will not solve the delinquency problem. The churches can furnish religious motivation to social workers, juvenile judges, and even police officers. Someone has said that the social problems confronting the Christian conscience require "a sociologist plus God, a social worker plus God, a psychiatrist plus God, a social engineer plus God."

The churches have been slow to recognize their role in helping meet the problem of juvenile delinquency. A rather typical attitude of many Christians, including religious leaders, was recently expressed in a conference for ministers on the problem of alcoholism. One pastor stood up to declare, "All this talk about the treatment of alcoholism may be good, but the only thing an alcoholic needs is to get Jesus Christ into his heart!" No Christian would question the absolute necessity of personal regeneration for alcoholics or juvenile delinquents. But our responsibility for them cannot be dismissed with a mere statement. The saving grace of God must be brought to bear upon the social order as well as upon the individual life. It is not good judgment to pull a man out of a burning building, win him to Christ, then thrust him back into the fire! The Christian gospel is set to save and to conserve people; it also has as its aim the evangelization of every area of our common life. The Christian lives under a mandate from his Lord to carry the gospel into the social order as well as to the individual.

If our crime-infested culture is the matrix out of which juvenile delinquency arises, then we must change the culture to make it more favorable to the growth and development of youth. We can drain off the moral swamps, clear the infested areas, make available low-rent housing that is fit for our future citizens, and reduce or eliminate those hazards for children, such as open vice and the sale of liquor, narcotics, and pornographic materials. If the church is the social conscience of the community, she will be concerned about health and recreational facilities, about better housing for blighted areas, and about the moral level of the community. The minister will proclaim the Christian message to the community, seeking to inform and inspire his people to action in the matter of delinquency.

The recovery of moral idealism will bring a respect for standards of honesty and truthfulness, reverence for property and life, and appreciation for law and authority. No one will question the earnest attempts to train and equip policemen and judges and social workers to help the youth who are in trouble. Christian compassion includes the best corrective care for society's offenders with a view to their rehabilitation. Several years ago, however, Walter Rauschenbusch saw the wisdom of turning off the faucet instead of trying to mop up all the water on the kitchen floor. In the case of juvenile crime, preventive measures are preferable to cures.

Another way of saving our youth is through the strengthening of the American home. The recovery of Christian ideals within the family will help to conserve marriage, prevent divorce, and insure the highest welfare of the child. It is the task of our churches to interpret the Christian teaching concerning marriage and the family,[9] to de-

[9] Matt. 5:27–32; 19:3–12; Mark 10:2–12; 1 Cor. 7; Eph. 5:22–33.

clare the biblical basis for discipline in the home,[10] and
to maintain a pastoral ministry designed to stabilize family
relations. The type of physical surroundings is important;
a living wage is necessary; love and affection are indis-
pensable. A home where children are given approval,
status, security, and affection becomes the training ground
for constructive, law-abiding citizens.

The churches can strengthen the spiritual foundations of
the family by encouraging worship and religious instruc-
tion and by bringing the gospel to bear upon the lives of
unregenerate people. Some of the best students of juvenile
delinquency see a correlation between regular church attendance and the problem of delinquency. J. Edgar
Hoover of the F. B. I. declares that the Sunday school is
a "powerful medium in materially reducing the army of
youthful offenders and delinquents." L. J. Carr, Director of
the Child Guidance Institute and professor of sociology
at the University of Michigan, says that if the churches
would reach the unchurched, "the high percentage of delinquent children, who have little or no religious training,
would automatically take care of itself." [11]

The religion of Jesus Christ must become a vital factor
in our morally desolate homes. He who came to make all
things new can change human nature, check human selfishness, bring sanity to the social order, and unite church
and home in a crusade to save our youth from serious
trouble. Any society that undertakes to conserve its youth
will have its reward. "Take this child . . . and I will give
thee thy wages." [12]

[10] Prov. 13:24; 22:6, 15; Eph. 6:1–4; Col. 3:20–21.
[11] Quoted by H. H. Barnett, "The Role of the Church in the Conservation of Youth," *The Review and Expositor*, XLVII. (April, 1950),
p. 176.
[12] Exodus 2:9.

13

Caesar Is Not Dead

H. GUY MOORE

In the year 60 B.C. Julius Caesar started a climb to supreme power over other contenders for the crown that was to be final and undisputed—or so he thought.

In his interesting book *The Spiritual Values in Shakespeare* Ernest Marshall Howse makes this significant comment on Caesar's tenuous rise and fall.

The superstitions of ancient days made a special divinity to hedge a king. On February 15, 44 B.C., the subservient senate tendered Caesar a crown. Caesar declined; but he seemed to observers "very loath to lay his fingers off it." A month later the rumor ran that he was to receive a second offer. As he was proceeding to the Senate House, a group of his enemies, incited by Cassius, closed in and stabbed him to death. Immediately, a rival group, headed by Anthony, fomented a civil war to seize power for themselves.

Coming events cast their shadows before. Even in the play one can foresee the inevitable sequence: *a second Caesar, more tyrannous than the first.* Selfish and unscrupulous men supporting movements professedly in the name of freedom created a malignant chaos that destroyed freedom.[1]

So it would be, said Anthony in his famous oration:

> I come to bury Caesar, not to praise him.
> The evil that men do lives after them;
> The good is oft interred with their bones.

[1] Abingdon Press, 1955, p. 91–92.

116

Caesar would not be buried. The evil would live on. "A second Caesar more tyrannous than the first" would take the throne. And the greatest champion of human freedom ever to live would be baited for the trap of bondage.

Thus came the Pharisees with their "nauseous flattery" and their obvious subtlety to catch Jesus on the horns of a dilemma. "Tell us, therefore, what thinkest thou? Is it lawful to give tribute unto Caesar, or not?" The question was so cleverly and maliciously framed that if Jesus answered either "yes" or "no" they would have him. If he said "pay the tax," he would be siding with Rome against his own people. If he said "no," he would immediately be tried for treason against Rome. What would he do? How would he answer?

Jesus made no effort to evade the issue. He was not caught in a corner. He knew the answer. He knew where a man's allegiance belonged. He knew what place all men hold under the sovereignty of God. His answer was clear, positive, forthright: "Render therefore unto Caesar the things which are Caesar's; and unto God the things that are God's."

In that statement we have the clearest enunciation of the principle of separation of church and state ever uttered. Jesus said clearly, "Pay the tax." But he said it with an inescapable logic. The coin, with its likeness and inscription, was for him as for others a recognized symbol that the country was living under Roman rule. He may well have thought, as some now think, that some payment was reasonably due the government for its services to order and protection. Yet that was the smallest part of the answer. The major and unexpected part was the duty of rendering to God his just due of worship and repentance and obedience. That, in any political setting, was still the supreme claim on people. In substance the Master was saying: "There are certain obligations which a citizen owes to the state. They must be met. There are other obligations which one owes to God alone. Over these the state has no right whatsoever."

I. VOICES OF FREEDOM

Taking their stand on this principle of our Lord, Christians across the centuries have endeavored to follow that dual loyalty. In their lives God's "good" has lived on in spite of Caesar's evil.

Let it be said in all candor and honest humility, it has not been easy. What belongs to Caesar and what belongs to God have not always been simple to determine. History bears out Dr. Halford Luccock's observation.

The meaning of the words "Render to Caesar the things that are Caesar's, and to God the things that are God's," is for all time what it was when Jesus spoke them. Unfortunately, however, they have been as badly twisted as any he every uttered. . . . The words have been distorted into a divine injunction to support any government, no matter how unjust, vicious, and oppressive. They have been cited even as giving Jesus' blessing to that disastrous separation between political conduct and religious conduct which has resulted in the "split personality" of Christians and churches—everybody trying to keep his religion, which is God's realm, out of his politics, which is Caesar's.[2]

The church is no less guilty than the state, for it too has at times claimed too much power—seating and unseating

[2] From *The Interpreter's Bible* (Nashville: Abingdon-Cokesbury Press, 1951–56), Vol. VII, p. 840.

civil rulers, selling its services, holding its people in virtual ignorance and slavery that it might hold absolute authority over every area of life.

Ever and again man in his unfolding history has come to the realization that his soul-freedom is not a right granted by the state or any human power but an inherent, inalienable right bestowed upon him because he was so made in the image of his Creator. His first allegiance, therefore, belongs to God. No human agency or power has a right to deny him that freedom and that allegiance.

It was this conviction that dominated the words and actions of Christ's first followers when they faced a conflict in allegiance. Commanded by men to refrain from preaching the gospel, they answered, "Whether it be right in the sight of God to hearken unto you more than unto God, judge ye. For we cannot but speak the things which we have seen and heard."

This, too, was back of the decision of the Christians of those early centuries. They refused to fight Caesar's battle or otherwise identify themselves with his cause even though they knew it would result in bitter persecution.

In the first-century world, Christianity was the only religion that refused to identify itself with the state, or to regard the voice of Caesar as the voice of God. In those early days religion and nationalism were synonymous terms. Men thought that to be loyal to their country was to be loyal to their God; to serve the state was to serve God. Every religion in that early period was definitely attached to some nation. The single exception to this rule was Christianity, which by its very nature could not be exclusively identified with the fortunes of any one nation. Indeed, the unwillingness of the early Christians to identify their religion with the fortunes of the state, excluded them from the tolerant attitude which Rome maintained toward other religions, and made them subject to suspicion, if not persecution.[3]

It was the desire for freedom of the conscience that gave birth to the Protestant Reformation. The basic idea of the Reformation was the challenge of the Roman Catholic doctrine of "the church" as the custodian of grace, the authoritative interpreter of God's Word, the doorway into the Kingdom, the arbiter of man's relation to God, and the supreme dictator of policy to the government. Martin Luther challenged the right of the church to grant indulgences for sin, and later challenged the whole traditional authority of the Roman Church. When he stood before the Diet of Worms, Luther echoed Peter's courage: "I cannot do otherwise. God help me!"

The passing years would not dim the light. The oppression of the state and the state church in the old world was the tempest that filled the sails and drove the ships toward the new world and a new freedom.

How briefly and yet how clearly does Dr. Walter Pope Binns, president of William Jewell College and one of the ablest proponents of religious freedom, state it.

It remained for America in modern times to establish religious liberty and to promulgate the doctrine of separation of church and state. This distinctive contribution of America to the science of government is one in which the Baptists have played a prominent part. Roger Williams and his associates implemented the doctrine when they established in Rhode Island the first civil government in the world that guaranteed to its inhabitants absolute religious freedom.

The historic battle for religious liberty came in the next

[3] Harold Cooke Phillips, *Life's Unanswered Questions* (New York: Harper and Brothers, 1944), p. 141.

century when Thomas Jefferson, James Madison and George Mason received hearty support from the Baptists as they challenged the establishment of religion in Virginia. This contest resulted in the adoption in 1785 of the Statute of Virginia for Religious Freedom, an achievement which Jefferson commemorated in the famous epitaph which he wrote for his own tomb.

With the example of the noble experiment in Rhode Island, and following the long and scholarly debate in Virginia, it was only natural that the guarantee of religious liberty and the principle of separation of church and state should finally be written into the fundamental law of the land in the form of the First Amendment to the Constitution adopted in 1790. Again it was Jefferson who clearly enunciated the principle when he said: "Religion is a matter which lies solely between man and his God: He owes account to none other for his faith or for his worship. The legislative powers of government reach actions only, and not opinions. I contemplate with sovereign reverence that act of the whole American people which declared that the Legislature should make no law respecting an establishment of religion, or prohibiting the free exercise thereof," thus building a wall of separation between church and state.[4]

So have they spoken across the centuries echoing and re-echoing his immortal principle: "Render therefore unto Caesar the things which are Caesar's; and unto God the things that are God's." It has become so much a part of our way of life that today America stands as the foremost champion in the world for the cause of religious freedom and separation of church and state.

II. THE LIVING ISSUE

There is, however, the ever present danger that we may in fatal complacency succumb to the mistaken belief that

[4] "Religious Liberty—A Baptist Interpretation," pamphlet published by Baptist Joint Public Affairs Committee.

"Caesar is dead" and that the "evil he would do does *not* live after him." Men have committed that tragic error before—believing that some victory for good has been final.

Caesar does not die easily. His wants are not easily satisfied. No generation is without his presence, reaching out with insatiable greed and selfishness to lay claim to that which is not his.

The issue of the separation of church and state involving the freedom of men's souls is today a living issue.

At this very hour the Southern Baptist secretary of mission work in Latin America is in Colombia to see what is back of the outburst of persecution against those whose only crime is asking for the right to worship God according to their conscience and to preach the gospel of Christ according to what they believe to be the leadership of the Holy Spirit.

Nor is the issue dead even here in America. Let us never forget that some share the blessings of our freedom but do not share the conviction that there must always be a wall of separation between church and state. Indeed, there are many indications that Roman Catholics are working tirelessly to breach that wall.

In a recent article Dr. J. M. Dawson points up a number of trends and dangers centering particularly in our national capital toward the "mixing of our allegiances." Among them is what he calls "a growing practice—particularly transparent patronage—in the disposition of Congressmen to provide benefits to the churches by loopholes in legislation. Sometimes this is open, allowing hospitals owned and controlled by churches admittedly religious in character, to qualify for huge sums of tax monies.

"In many instances the bills providing benefits to the churches make use of phrases which hide their benefits at the time they are voted. In other cases, by the omission of a single word 'public,' church schools could qualify for millions in aid." Such action, wittingly or unwittingly, is a direct violation of the principle of the separation of church and state.

It would be less than Christian of us here in America if we, enjoying our own cherished freedom, forget those yet in one kind of bondage or another around the world. We dare not ignore the plea of men like Dr. Gunnar Westin, professor of history and philosophy at Uppsala University, Sweden, and speaker at the Baptist World Congress in London in 1955.

There is nothing that can set a Baptist gathering so on fire as oppression and violence in religious matters. Baptists have, during the last 400 years, given full evidence of this. They have preached and taught religious liberty; they have demanded it, fought for it, practiced it under severe persecutions, and eagerly defended it against the mighty powers of this world.

This fight is not ended. We must rise in protest against state and church authorities which have not learned to know freedom of conscience and the human right to worship in liberty. We are called upon to oppose such powers today which openly violate freedom in various respects, and especially the freedom of religious belief and practice.

It was in answer to such appeals that the historic "Declaration on Religious Liberty" was adopted by the Baptist World Congress. These words from the preamble are significant: "Assembled in London, England, in the Year of our Lord 1955, at the Golden Jubilee Congress of the Baptist World Alliance, and gathered from all parts of the world, we are aware not only of our common Christian heritage as Baptists, but also of the fear, the conflicts, and the tyranny of force which are notable features of our modern world. We who believe in a loving God and belong to the kingdom of Christ, would reaffirm those fundamental Christian principles of freedom which our forefathers proclaimed at great cost, but to the enrichment of civilization and of the church.

"As Baptists we are aware that the battle for religious liberty still goes on. We see at this time a recurrence of persecution, intolerance, and enforced uniformity of conduct and thought. A creeping peril menaces freedom, basic human values, even Christianity itself." No, Caesar is not dead. He still lays claim to that which rightfully belongs to God.

III. THE DREAM MUST NOT DIE

It is up to us, therefore, to see to it that the "good" for which our fathers lived and died be not buried with them. We can and must keep the dream alive. Our text is not an invitation to be against something. It is a challenge to be for something. Jesus was recognizing a solemn and sincere obligation when he said, "Render unto Caesar the things that are Caesar's."

Insofar as our nation is carrying out its functions of "a government of the people, by the people, and for the people" under God, we should give to it our loyalty, our love, our fullest support. Let it be said of us: "The love of the Christian for his people should . . . be part of his gratitude to God for the riches which are his through the community into which he has been born. Each generation has inherited from the past a distinctive . . . culture by which its own mind and character have been shaped. Of this it is a trustee rather than an owner. It is its duty to preserve that inheritance and to transmit it unimpaired and if possible enhanced to posterity." [5]

Too long have we Americans taken the best from our nation's life and given back the worst. Too long have we reserved the right to criticize and also the right to be indifferent and complacent. Caesar has done us evil because we have been too careless about the kind of man we elect to be his spokesman.

Even Christians have allowed this separation of allegiance to breed a kind of departmentalized religion. In one realm Caesar has been king and in another Christ—if such be possible—and never the twain have met.

Caesar has taken title not only to government but to business, to home, to pleasure, and to just about everything else. Whatever is left is God's. God has been neatly and conveniently kept in his own sphere—which in many cases means church on Sunday morning!

The nation, strong under God, waits for men who are Christian in business, in the home, in the school, and in government—men willing to give their best in redeemed character and Christian service. Their loyalty to their nation is clean and good and strong because they know a higher loyalty. They have learned how to say with Christ, "Render unto Caesar the things which are Caesar's"—but first and last and always, "unto God the things that are God's."

In the spirit of all who have gone before and for the sake of all who shall come after us let us by God's grace pledge ourselves to keep that dream, God's dream, alive.

[5] Ernest Fremont Tittle, *The Gospel According to Luke* (New York: Harper and Brothers, 1951), p. 215.

14

A Charter of Christian Living

PHILIPPIANS 4:8–9

OLIN T. BINKLEY

The climate of thought in American society is changing. There is a resurgence of interest in the spiritual foundations of life, and people are turning to the churches for moral guidance.

A creative minority of church members are thinking seriously about the vital issues in our divided and frightened world, and they are asking penetrating questions. What is the Christian ideal of personal character? What are the moral principles of Christian action? How does Jesus Christ desire his disciples to think, speak, and act in our complex and changing social order? How can we translate faith into deed?

This quest for moral insight and courage draws us to a fresh study of the Bible. When we read the New Testament with teachable minds and tender hearts, we hear the call of the Master to seek first the kingdom of God and his righteousness. We learn how to examine human problems in the perspective of the sovereignty of God. We discover that the direction of Christian action in concrete situations is to be determined by reference to what God has done for us in Christ. We receive stimulus to develop a mature sense of moral responsibility, to order our lives by the ethic of justice and love which our Lord set out to estab-

126

lish on earth, and to participate in the adventure of Christian living in this revolutionary age.

It is not enough for us to celebrate the moral victories won by former generations. We must take a stand on the main issues confronting the moral conscience now, and we need the type of Christian wisdom discoverable in Paul's message to the Philippians. Listen to his words: "Finally, brethren, whatsoever things are true, whatsoever things are honorable, whatsoever things are just, whatsoever things are pure, whatsoever things are lovely, whatsoever things are of good report; if there be any virtue, and if there be any praise, think on these things. The things which ye both learned and received and heard and saw in me, these things do: and the God of peace shall be with you" (Phil. 4:8–9 ASV).

I. A PLEA FOR CLEAR ETHICAL PERCEPTION

The first element of this charter of Christian living is an earnest plea for moral discrimination: "think on these things." Paul urged the disciples of Jesus at Philippi, whom he loved and trusted, to use their minds honestly and persistently in the conduct of life. He counseled them to concentrate upon truth, justice, and love. He wanted them to test every proposal by moral criteria. Is it true? Is it honorable? Is it just? Is it pure? Is it the lovely thing to do? Is it a course of action which is held in honor by good men?

In this appeal for Christian thinking on fundamental issues there is no blurring of the distinction between right and wrong. Paul was deeply convinced that dishonesty, injustice, hatred, and cruelty are morally wrong. He affirmed the powerful conviction that truth, honor, justice, purity, and love are the principles of right action. Guided by these ideals, we can distinguish the things that differ.

We can raise the banner of personal purity and social righteousness in the Christian community. We can evaluate the proposals of pressure groups and approve whatever is morally excellent.

Dr. T. R. Glover has said that the Christian church refused to compromise in the Roman Empire and won a decisive victory because the disciples of Jesus "out-thought, out-lived, and out-died the pagans." In memory of those wise and brave pioneers, let us listen gratefully and obediently to what the Holy Spirit is saying to the churches today. Let us keep thinking about truth, justice, and love, and about the relation of these principles to the problems confronting us each day in the family, in economic life, and in race relations. It is not easy to define justice in these particular social contexts, and we need all the light and help we can get from the Bible and from social science.

At this hour in the history of American civilization it is appropriate to read the addresses of Pericles as reported by Thucydides in the *History of the Peloponnesian War*. In one speech Pericles urged the Athenians to go to war and pointed out their superior wealth, unity, naval skill, and power. A few months later he spoke at a public funeral at Athens for the citizens who had fallen in battle during the first summer of the war. In the funeral oration he did not mention their possessions. He did not recount their military victories. Instead he declared that the true greatness of the Athenians was to be ascribed to their principles of freedom, equality of rights, justice, and generosity.

The United States has become a center of economic power, scientific skill, and literary vitality; and we have won victories over formidable and implacable adversaries. But the moral latitude is wide in this country, and although there is much that is noble and good, there is also much that is flatly at variance with the spirit and teaching of Jesus. Measured by the standards of the New Testament the moral level of the churches is unquestionably low. The South has been called the Bible belt, but the crime rates of Southern cities are the highest in the nation. Recent demonstrations of hatred, deception, and cruelty remind us that the society in which we live is far less Christian in its basic presuppositions and motivations than the rising tide of church membership might indicate.

If there is to be any moral excellence in our homes and communities, we shall have to keep thinking about whatever is true, honorable, just, pure, lovely, and of good report; and we shall have to combine the best intelligence with the highest devotion to Christ in the main stream of life both in the rural counties and in the growing cities of our restless society.

II. A CALL TO CHRISTIAN ACTION

The second element of this charter of Christian living is a clear call to constructive action: "these things do." The God revealed in Jesus Christ has taken costly action "for us men and our salvation," and he calls us to active service on the frontiers of strife in contemporary society. He leads us along the Christian path of ethical perception, firm decision, and faithful work. Apart from him we can do nothing, but by his grace and help we "can do all things" (Phil. 4:13).

We understand that our abilities and our opportunities for service are limited. We are limited by heredity and by the culture in which we live. We are limited by the "systems" through which we function: the wage system, the price system, the transportation system, the tax system. We are limited by our time in history and by a relatively short span of life. We are limited by our own imperfections and sins. We are limited—but we are not helpless! If we respond affirmatively to God's upward call in Christ and use the available resources, we *can* do some things which are worth doing.

1. *We can develop the kind of personal character that will stand the strain of responsible living in a dynamic society.* If we humbly seek to know and to do God's will, we shall be sustained by a power that is stronger than the stresses of modern civilization. Christ will dwell in our hearts by faith, and we shall grow in Christian maturity.

There is a vital relation between Christlike character and effective action. Listen again to Paul's persuasive words to his dear friends at Philippi: "The things which ye both learned and received and heard and saw in me, these things do." What had they seen in him? They had seen in Paul the qualities of a man completely committed to Christ: a deep knowledge of God, a genuine concern for the lost, a strong courage in the presence of peril, and a willingness to suffer in a good cause. Blessed is the man who possesses this kind of character in the twentieth century. He will be able to stand the strain of life and to do "that which is good toward all men, and especially toward them that are of the household of the faith" (Gal. 6:10 ASV).

2. *We can participate in the advancement of the gospel of Christ in this generation.* Paul thanked the Christians at Philippi for their participation in the progress of the gospel from the first day he proclaimed the message in Europe and assured them that everything that had happened to him, including imprisonment, had really served to advance the gospel. Now you and I have an opportunity to be "fellow workmen for God," devoting the creative energies of our

lives to the redemptive work of the churches in human society. The gospel has not lost its power to win men and to transform them, and we have been commissioned to "make disciples" of all nations, teaching them to obey the moral imperatives of the Christian faith. In this task, as John Oman said, we are concerned with "what is best worth appreciating," and adventurous in "what is best worth doing."

3. *We can stand on the front line of Christian conscience in the community in which we live.* One of the profoundest moral concepts in the New Testament relates to the responsibility of Christian citizenship. Paul was interpreting the mind of Christ for the Christian community at Philippi when he said, "Only let your manner of life be worthy of the gospel of Christ." Precisely what was Paul saying? He was saying to those first-century Christians, "You are committed to the moral ideals of Christ. You are responsible members of the society in which you live. You are under obligation to behave as citizens in a way that is worthy of the gospel of Christ."

This message is desperately needed among Christians in the United States today. There has been a vigorous, persistent movement of people into the churches within recent years, but the moral tone of the common life is not clear and strong. This is the hour for us to recover the moral message of the Christian faith and to declare the truth that every person saved by grace through faith is committed to the Christian way of life in his family, his vocation, and his community. The principles of Christian social action are freedom, fellowship, and service. Are we guiding our political and economic decisions by these principles? Is our behavior in race relations worthy of the gospel of Christ? Are we working with wisdom, humility, and courage for a truly democratic society? This is our moral task as Christians in a disordered world.

III. A PROMISE

The third element of this charter of Christian living is a promise: "the God of peace shall be with you." Paul confronts us with the loftiest ideals and challenges us to undertake great things for Christ. Then he gives us one assurance: the peace of God, which transcends human understanding, will guard our minds and hearts.

This promise is at the heart of Christian truth. The God of righteousness and love goes with his children on every difficult and dangerous assignment. He often does not remove our burdens, but he gives us courage to face them. He often does not relax our tensions, but he is with us in our time of trouble. The sense of his nearness fills our hearts with love, joy, and peace and enables us to face the future with confidence and hope.

In these epochal years of social change Paul's promise holds good. There is opposition to our ethical aspirations, but the God of peace is with us. He gives us wisdom for sound decisions and power for responsible action. He calls us to our knees for worship and then to our feet for service. And as the light of eternity falls upon our passing days, the light of his truth and love illuminates every step of the way.

About the Writers

Dr. Theodore F. Adams, pastor, First Baptist Church, Richmond, Virginia, is a native of New York. He is a graduate of Denison University (B.A.) and Rochester Theological Seminary (B.D.). For twelve years he was pastor of churches in Ohio before moving in 1936 to his present pastorate in Virginia. He served for ten years as a member of the Southern Baptist Foreign Mission Board and is now a trustee of the University of Richmond, chairman of the Board of Trustees, Virginia Union University, and president of the Baptist World Alliance. Dr. Adams lectures frequently on marriage and the home, and he has written *Making Your Marriage Succeed*.

Dr. Olin T. Binkley, since 1952, has been professor of Christian sociology and ethics, Southeastern Baptist Theological Seminary at Wake Forest in his native North Carolina. His educational background includes Wake Forest College (B.A.), Southern Baptist Theological Seminary (Th.B.), Yale Divinity School (B.D.), and Yale University (Ph.D.). He previously served as pastor of the Chapel Hill Baptist Church, as head of the Department of Religion at Wake Forest College, and as professor of ethics and sociology at Southern Seminary. Dr. Binkley holds membership in the American Sociological Society, the American Association of Marriage Counselors, and Phi Beta Kappa and is the author of *Frontiers for Christian Youth* and *The Churches and the Social Conscience*.

Dr. Nolan P. Howington, pastor, First Baptist Church, Little Rock, Arkansas, is a native of Georgia and holds the B.A. and M.A. degrees from Wake Forest College and the Th.M. and Th.D. degrees from Southern Baptist Theological Seminary. He has been a chaplain in the U. S. Army, has taught sociology at Carson-Newman College, and has been pastor of churches in North Carolina and Tennessee before assuming his present pastorate in 1953. Dr. Howington received the Bronze Star Medal during World War II, and he holds membership in the American Sociological Society, the Academy of Political and Social Sciences, and the National Council on Family Relations.

133

Dr. R. Lofton Hudson, pastor, Wornall Road Baptist Church, Kansas City, Missouri, since 1950, is a native of Tennessee. He earned the B.S. and Ph.D. degrees at George Peabody College, the Th.B. at Southern Baptist Seminary, and the M.A. at Vanderbilt University. Previous pastorates were at Portland and Chattanooga, Tennessee, and at Shawnee, Oklahoma. Dr. Hudson's extensive writings include numerous articles for periodicals; a weekly column, "Counselor's Corner," published in ten state Baptist papers; and four books: *The Religion of a Sound Mind, The Religion of a Mature Person, Taproots for Tall Souls,* and *Growing a Christian Personality.*

Dr. Carlyle Marney, pastor, First Baptist Church, Austin, Texas, since 1948, is a native of Tennessee. He received the A.B. degree from Carson-Newman College and the Th.M. and Th.D. degrees from Southern Baptist Theological Seminary. He is guest professor of homiletics at Austin Presbyterian Theological Seminary, has been preaching missioner to numerous Army and Air Force bases at home and abroad, has been preacher or lecturer on more than thirty college campuses, and conducts weekly radio and television programs. Dr. Marney's books include two volumes, *Any Man's Family* and *Mothers and Sons,* from his television series and *These Things Remain.*

Dr. H. Guy Moore, pastor, Broadway Baptist Church, Fort Worth, Texas, is a native of Illinois and was educated at William Jewell College (B.A.) and Southern Baptist Theological Seminary (Th.M.). For thirteen years he was pastor of churches in St. Louis and Kansas City, Missouri, before moving to Fort Worth in 1947. A member of the Southern Baptist Home Mission Board and of the Committee on World Evangelization, a contributor to publications of the Convention's Sunday School Board, a frequent speaker at assemblies and college religious emphasis weeks, Dr. Moore has traveled extensively and in 1955 was a speaker at the Baptist World Alliance in London, England.

Dr. Jack R. Noffsinger, pastor, First Baptist Church, Gainesville, Florida, received his formal education at the University of Richmond and Colgate-Rochester Theological Seminary. He served three years as a Navy chaplain and at the age of twenty-eight became pastor of the Tabernacle Baptist Church of Richmond, Virginia, where he remained until 1951 when he was called to the Florida church. He is a member of the Southern Baptist Radio and Television Commission. He has spoken during many college religious emphasis weeks and to numerous student conventions and assemblies. Dr. Noffsinger is a member of Phi Beta Kappa.

Dr. Arthur B. Rutledge, pastor, First Baptist Church, Marshall, Texas, since 1945, is a native of San Antonio, Texas. His educational background includes Baylor University (B.A.) and Southern Baptist Theological Seminary (Th.M. and Th.D.). He is the author of *Homes That Last*, a Baptist Training Union study course book. Dr. Rutledge has served Southern Baptists both as a member of the Radio and Television Commission and as a member of the Foreign Mission Board. He was chairman of the Texas Baptist Christian Life Commission, 1951–1955, and is now chairman of the Executive Board of the Baptist General Convention of Texas.

Dr. Scott L. Tatum, pastor, Broadmoor Baptist Church, Shreveport, in his native state of Louisiana, holds the B.A. degree from Baylor University and the Th.M. and Th.D. degrees from Southwestern Baptist Theological Seminary. He has been pastor of churches in Canton, Hubbard, and Austin in Texas for ten years before going to Louisiana in 1951. In addition to widespread speaking engagements, Dr. Tatum has served as moderator of the Caddo Baptist Association and is now a member of the board of trustees of Southwestern Seminary and vice-president of the Louisiana Baptist Convention.

Dr. Charles A. Trentham is pastor of the First Baptist Church of Knoxville in his native Tennessee. He holds the B.A. degree from Carson-Newman College, the Th.M. and Th.D. degrees from Southwestern Baptist Theological Seminary, and the Ph.D. degree from the University of Edinburgh. His denominational responsibilities include membership on the Baptist Sunday School Board. Dr. Trentham has taught in the department of religion at Baylor University and in the School of Religion, University of Tennessee. Before assuming his present position he was head of the department of systematic theology at Southwestern Baptist Theological Seminary.

Dr. J. B. Weatherspoon, professor of preaching, Southern Baptist Theological Seminary, Louisville, Kentucky, is a native of North Carolina. He earned the A.B. and M.A. degrees at Wake Forest College and then the Th.M. and Th.D. degrees from Southern Baptist Theological Seminary. After more than a decade of pastoral experience in North Carolina and Kentucky, he became in 1927 a member of Southern Seminary's faculty. In 1929 he was elected professor of homiletics and sociology there. Dr. Weatherspoon has written extensively, served his denomination in various capacities including the chairmanship first of the Social Service Commission and then of the Christian Life Commission, and is listed in *Who's Who in America.*

Rev. Charles Wellborn, pastor, Seventh and James Baptist Church, Waco, Texas, since 1951, is a native Texan and holds the B.A. and M.A. degrees from Baylor University as well as the B.D. degree from Southwestern Baptist Theological Seminary. As a college student he was twice National Intercollegiate Debating Champion and once National Oratorical Champion. He served three years in the American Army Ski Troops and then was a Baylor University faculty member in the departments of religion and political science. He has preached in many city-wide youth revivals and other evangelistic campaigns across the South. For three years he was the speaker on the Southern Baptist Convention's "Baptist Hour" radio program.

Dr. William R. White, president, Baylor University, Waco, Texas, since 1948, holds the A.B. degree from Howard Payne College, and the Th.M. and Th.D. degrees from Southwestern Baptist Theological Seminary. Among his pastorates are Broadway Baptist Church, Fort Worth, First Baptist Church, Oklahoma City, and First Baptist Church, Austin. He has filled the following posts of denominational responsibility: professor of missions, Southwestern Seminary; executive secretary, Baptist General Convention of Texas; president, Hardin Simmons University; and editorial secretary, Baptist Sunday School Board. Dr. White has written extensively, has served by Presidential appointment since 1951 as a member of the International Development Advisory Board (Point 4), and is listed in *Who's Who in America.*

Dr. J. Howard Williams, president, Southwestern Baptist Theological Seminary, Fort Worth, Texas, is a native of Texas. His educational background includes Baylor University (B.A.) and Southwestern Seminary (Th.M.). His best known pastorates have been the First Baptist Church of Amarillo, Texas, and the First Baptist Church of Oklahoma City. In his five-year ministry in the latter church there were more than 600 additions per year. In addition to having served on the executive committees of the Southern Baptist Convention and the Baptist World Alliance, Dr. Williams served for thirteen years during two different terms as executive secretary of the Baptist General Convention of Texas.